Lecture Notes in Computer Science　9231

Commenced Publication in 1973
Founding and Former Series Editors:
Gerhard Goos, Juris Hartmanis, and Jan van Leeuwen

More information about this series at http://www.springer.com/series/7407

Yunji Chen · Paolo Ienne
Qing Ji (Eds.)

Advanced Parallel Processing Technologies

11th International Symposium, APPT 2015
Jinan, China, August 20–21, 2015
Proceedings

 Springer

Editors
Yunji Chen
Chinese Academy of Sciences
Beijing
China

Qing Ji
Inspur
Shangdong
China

Paolo Ienne
EPFL IC ISIM LAP
Lausanne
Switzerland

ISSN 0302-9743   ISSN 1611-3349   (electronic)
Lecture Notes in Computer Science
ISBN 978-3-319-23215-7   ISBN 978-3-319-23216-4   (eBook)
DOI 10.1007/978-3-319-23216-4

Library of Congress Control Number: 2015946764

LNCS Sublibrary: SL1 – Theoretical Computer Science and General Issues

Springer Cham Heidelberg New York Dordrecht London

Printed on acid-free paper

Springer International Publishing AG Switzerland is part of Springer Science+Business Media
(www.springer.com)

Preface

The ever-increasing demand of parallel processing drives society to investigate new computer architecture and system software techniques. Following this trend, APPT 2015 broadly captured the recent advances in big data processing, parallel architectures and systems, parallel software, parallel algorithms and applications, distributed and cloud computing, etc., and provided an excellent forum for the presentation of research efforts and the exchange of viewpoints.

We would like to express our gratitude to all the colleagues who submitted papers and congratulate those whose papers were accepted. Following the successes in the previous 20 years, APPT managed to provide a high-quality program for all attendees. Among 24 submissions, the Program Committee (PC) decided to accept eight papers, with a acceptance rate of 33.3 %. Most submissions were reviewed by three PC members. There was also an online discussion stage to guarantee that consensus was reached for each submission.

While we would like to thank the authors for submitting their fine work to APPT 2015, and we would also like to show our sincere appreciation to this year's PC. The 30 PC members did an excellent job in returning high-quality reviews in time and engaging in a constructive online discussion. We would also like to thank the general chairs (Prof. Endong Wang and Yong Dou), the Organizing Committee members, the publicity and exhibition chairs, and publication chairs. The contributions from our sponsors and supporters were also invaluable: We would like to thank the China Computer Federation, the Technical Committee on Computer Architecture of the China Computer Federation, the National Laboratory for Parallel and Distributed Processing, the State Key Laboratory of Computer Architecture, and the State Key Laboratory of High-End Server and Storage Technology. Our thanks also go to Springer for its assistance in putting the proceedings together. Finally, we offer our special thanks to the Inspur Company, which made APPT 2015 possible.

June 2015

Yunji Chen
Qing Ji
Paolo Ienne

Organization

APPT 2015 was organized by the China Computer Federation.

General Chairs

Endong Wang	Inspur, China
Yong Dou	National University of Defense Technology, China

Steering Committee Chair

Yong Dou	National University of Defense Technology, China

Steering Committee

Zhenzhou Ji	Harbin Institute of Technology, China
Dongsheng Wang	Tsinghua University, China
Xingwei Wang	Northeastern University, China
Minyou Wu	Shanghai Jiaotong University, China
Gongxuan Zhang	Nanjing University of Science and Technology, China
Junjie Wu	National University of Defense Technology, China

Organization Chairs

Weifeng Gong	Inspur, China
Zhiping Jia	Shandong University, China

Organizing Committee

Lei Ju	Shandong University, China
Xin Li	Shandong University, China
Yibin Li	Shandong University, China
Lizhao Liu	Inspur, China
Lu Lu	Inspur, China
Jiehui Si	Inspur, China

Program Chairs

Yunji Chen	Institute of Computing Technology Chinese Academy of Sciences, China
Paolo Ienne	Swiss Federal Institute of Technology in Lausanne, Switzerland
Qing Ji	Inspur, China

Program Committee

Yiran Chen	University of Pittsburgh, USA
Lizhong Chen	Oregon State University, USA
Albert Cohen	Inria, France
Reetuparan Das	Intel Labs, USA
Stijn Eyerman	Ghent University, Belgium
Michael Ferdman	Stony Brook University, USA
Junli Gu	AMD, China
Qi Guo	Carnegie Mellon University, USA
Wei Chung Hsu	National Chaio Tung University, China (Taiwan)
Weixing Ji	Beijing Institute of Technology, China
Guoliang Jin	North Carolina State University, USA
Wolfgang Karl	Karlsruhe Institute of Technology (KIT), Germany
Jangwoo Kim	POSTECH, Korea
John Kim	KAIST, Korea
Tao Li	University of Florida, USA
Xiaofei Liao	Huazhong University of Science and Technology, China
Felix Xiaozhu Lin	Purdue ECE, USA
Brandon Lucia	University of Washington, USA
Ozcan Ozturk	Bilkent University, Turkey
Thomas Pawlowski	Micron, USA
Smruti Sarangi	IIT, India
Rui Wang	Beihang University, China
Bo Wu	Colorado School of Mines, USA
Yuan Xie	University of California at Santa Barbara, USA
Yi Yang	NEC Laboratories America, USA
Pen-Chung Yew	University of Minnesota at Twin Cities, USA
Qing Yi	University of Colorado at Colorado Springs, USA
Zhibin Yu	Shenzhen Institute of Advanced Technology, China
Antonia Zhai	University of Minnesota, USA
Huiyang Zhou	NC State University, USA

Publicity and Exhibition Chairs

Yu Tao	Inspur, China
Wei Chen	National University of Defense of Technology, China

Publication Chairs

Junjie Wu	National University of Defense Technology, China
Dong Zhang	Inspur, China

Contents

Improving Memory Access Performance of In-Memory Key-Value Store
Using Data Prefetching Techniques 1
   PengFei Zhu, GuangYu Sun, Peng Wang, and MingYu Chen

DDC: Distributed Data Collection Framework for Failure Prediction
in Tianhe Supercomputers 18
   *Wei Hu, Yanhuang Jiang, Guangming Liu, Wenrui Dong,
   and Guilin Cai*

Optimizing the MapReduce Framework for CPU-MIC
Heterogeneous Cluster 33
   Wenzhu Wang, Qingbo Wu, Yusong Tan, and Yaoxue Zhang

Stable Matching Scheduler for Single-ISA Heterogeneous
Multi-core Processors 45
   *Lei Wang, Shaoli Liu, Chao Lu, Longbing Zhang, Junhua Xiao,
   and Jian Wang*

RPECA-Rumor Propagation Based Eventual Consistency
Assessment Algorithm 60
   Dong Zhang, Zhiyuan Su, Kaiyuan Qi, Guomao Xin, and Peng Wei

Efficient Implementation of MIPS Code Generator for the IonMonkey
JavaScript Compiler 73
   Tong Ren, Shuangbai Xue, Fei Peng, Qing Wang, and Xiang Gao

Effects of Quenched Disorder on Liquid Crystal: A Simulation
of Rough Cylinder Confinement 86
   Qing Ji

Visual Tracking Based on Convolutional Deep Belief Network 103
   Dan Hu, Xingshe Zhou, and Junjie Wu

Author Index 117

Improving Memory Access Performance of In-Memory Key-Value Store Using Data Prefetching Techniques

PengFei Zhu[1]([✉]), GuangYu Sun[2], Peng Wang[2], and MingYu Chen[1]

[1] ACSL, Institute of Computing Technology, Chinese Academy of Science, Beijing, China
{zhupengfei,cmy}@ict.ac.cn
[2] CECA, Peking University, Beijing, China
{gsun,wang_peng}@pku.edu.cn

Abstract. In-memory Key-Value stores (IMKVs) provide significantly higher performance than traditional disk-based counterparts. As memory technologies advance, IMKVs become practical for modern Big Data processing, which include financial services, e-commerce, telecommunication network, etc. Recently, various IMKVs have been proposed from both academia and industrial. In order to leverage high performance random access capability of main memory, most IMKVs employ hashing based index structures to retrieve data according to keys. Consequently, a regular memory access pattern can be observed in data retrieval from those IMKVs. Normally speaking, one access to index (hash table), which is also located in main memory, is followed by another memory access to value data. Such a regular access pattern provides a potential opportunity that data prefetching techniques can be employed to improve memory access efficiency for data retrieval in these IMKVs. Based on this observation, we explore various data prefetching techniques with proper architecture level modifications on memory controller considering trade-off between design overhead and performance. Specifically, we focus on two key design issues of prefetching techniques: (1) where to fetch data (i.e. data address)? and (2) how many data to fetch (i.e. data size)? Experimental results demonstrate that memory access performance can be substantially improved up to 35.4 %. In addition, we also demonstrate the overhead of prefetching on power consumption.

Keywords: In-memory key-value store · Data prefetching · Memory controller optimization

1 Introduction

As we have moved into the era of Big Data, a huge number of modern applications that relies on large-scale distributed storage systems have emerged. However, traditional relational database management systems (RDBMS) may be inefficient for many of them mainly due to the fact that features of RDBMS,

© Springer International Publishing Switzerland 2015
Y. Chen et al. (Eds.): APPT 2015, LNCS 9231, pp. 1–17, 2015.
DOI: 10.1007/978-3-319-23216-4_1

such as support of complicated SQL queries, are no longer necessary [4]. There-fore, the key-value (KV) store has become popular and been widely adopted in modern data centers to support various Internet-wide services. These well-known KV stores include BigTable [5], Cassandra [11], Dynamo [7], etc. Although these KV stores can provide higher performance and better scalability than traditional RDBMS, their performance is still limited by their underneath storage infrastruc-ture that is based on hard disk drives (HDD). Thus, in order to satisfy increasing performance requirement of modern applications, the so-called in-memory KV stores (IMKVs) have attracted attention of storage researchers [20].

IMKV normally refers to a Key-Value (KV) store that uses main memory for data storage rather than disk-based storage. As the access speed to main memory is several orders faster than that to disk storage, IMKVs are usually employed for storage systems where response time is critical. These systems are widely adopted in financial services, e-commerce, telecommunication network, etc. [16] Recently, IMKVs become more and more attractive mainly because of advances in memory technologies. On the one hand, the decreasing price per bit of DRAM technology makes it possible to employ IMKVs for modern Big Data applications. On the other hand, various non-volatile memory technologies have potential to improve durability in IMKVs. Consequently, many IMKVs have been proposed from both academia and industry, which demonstrate 10-100x performance improvements over traditional disk-storage counterparts [2,3,18].

Since data are maintained in main memory, the efficiency of data accesses to memory is important for performance of these IMKVs. Compared to disk storage (either HDDs or SSDs), main memory has an intrinsic advantage that it supports high performance random accesses. Thus, unlike disk storage based databases, many IMKVs prefer using hash function based index structure to speed up index processing. Using such a hash index structure, we observe that the access pattern to main memory become more regular than that to traditional databases. Specifically, for those key-value stores based on IMKVs, one memory access to index is followed by another memory access to value data. The data access pattern provides a potential opportunity that data prefetching can be leveraged to improve performance of data retrieval in these IMKVs.

In fact, prefetching techniques have been widely researched in memory architecture design to improve efficiency of data access. Today, commercial microprocessors are equipped data prefetch engines to improve performance of memory-intensive workloads [1,23]. Based on hardware prefetcher, previous works [9,14] evaluate accurate measurement of performance metrics by prefetch-ing technologies. The basic idea of prefetching is to predict data that may be accessed in future according to current states or execution history. Then, these data are loaded in advance into on-chip caches [25] or memory controller [28] to hide access latency. Obviously, the efficiency of prefetching relies on temporal or spatial locality of data access pattern to main memory. For data accesses in IMKVs, the regular access pattern enables the potential of employing prefetching techniques.

Through various different prefetching techniques, there are two major design issues in common. First, how to detect which data should be prefetched (e.g. prefetching address). Second, how many data should be loaded in prefetching (e.g. prefetching size). Previous approaches normally depend on execution states or history to predict prefetching address and prefetching size. However, it is not straightforward to directly apply existing techniques on IMKVs. In order to efficiently handle above design issues, we extensively explore data structures of IMKVs and propose several design techniques optimized for different working environments. The main contributions of this work are summarized as follows,

- With careful analysis of data accesses to in-memory KV stores, we reveal the fact that a regular access pattern can be observed, which can be leveraged for efficient data prefetching.
- Considering the data structure of KV stores, we propose a simple but efficient extension to memory controller to predict the prefetching size.
- In order to identify the prefetching address, we propose two techniques, which are suitable for different cases. The design trade-off between these two techniques is also analyzed.
- Comprehensive experimental results are provided to evaluate efficiency of applying our methods on a real in-memory KV stores.

2   Background and Motivation

In this section, we will present a brief review of data retrieval in hash-indexing based IMKVs using a state-of-art representative. In addition, we will reveal the fact that a regular access pattern to main memory can be observed.

In recent times, various IMKVs have become vital components in modern datacenter storages, including Memcached [2,18], Redis [3], MICA [15], MemC3 [8], and RAMCloud [22]. In these systems, all data are kept in DRAM at all times to provide the lowest possible storage latency for different applications. And most of these systems employ hashing based index structures as it provides a $O(1)$ lookup time. In the rest of this section, we will use RAMCloud as a representative example to introduce how hash indexing works [22].

RAMCloud adopts a simple key-value data model consisting of binary objects that are associated with variable-length keys. Each RAMCloud server contains a collection of objects stored in a log area of DRAM via a log-structured approach and a hash table that points to every live object. As shown in Fig. 1, objects can only be accessed by their keys. It means that every object operation (access) interacts with the hash table. For example, in a read request from a client, the server must use the hash table to locate the object in the in-memory log area.

RAMCloud uses an open hashing method, in which there is only one possible bucket for a specific object in the table. If a bucket is full, additional chained entries are allocated separately to store more object references in the same bucket. RAMCloud servers will have tens or hundreds of gigabytes of DRAM, but the size of each object is likely to be quite small (a few hundred bytes or less). Therefore, the hash table may contain tens or hundreds of millions of individual

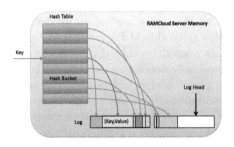

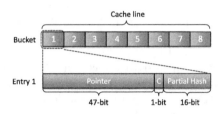

Fig. 1. Hash Table & Log in RAM-Cloud [22]

Fig. 2. Hash table bucket in RAM-Cloud.

entries. This means that the hash table working set is probably too large to be held in the processor's cache, and cache misses become unavoidable. RAMCloud expects each lookup will cause no more than two cache misses: one miss in the hash table bucket, and another to verify the key matches the object in log.

Several optimizations are applied in RAMCloud to reduce cache misses. As show in Fig. 2, each key is hashed into a specific bucket, which contains up to eight 47-bit direct pointers to objects within the in-memory log area. Each hash table bucket is aligned to a CPU cache line (64 bytes on current x86 processors, or eight hash entries). The hash table consists of a continuous array of such buckets. Accessing a bucket will often result in a cache miss, which loads a full cache line from memory. RAMCloud will then traverse all hash entries in the loaded cache line when doing a lookup.

To avoid retrieving each object referenced in the bucket in order to verify a match (i.e. to compare the key stored within the object in the log area), which would likely cause a cache miss, RAMCloud uses the upper 16 bits of each hash table pointer to store a partial hash of the key of the object referred. At this rate, if a bucket contains several valid entries, it is highly possible that at most one will have a matching partial hash in the bucket, so only one object will need to be accessed to compare the key. The remaining 47 bits are sufficient to locate the object within the in-memory log, and the 1-bit "C" flag indicates whether the bucket is chained due to overflow.

In summary, the most common memory access pattern in RAMCloud is: access one of hash table buckets, find one of hash entries in the bucket that matches the partial hash of the object's key, and then follow the pointer to retrieve the object in log area to compare the key and utilize the value of the object. It is confirmed by the memory trace we collected using Pin instrumentation tool [17].

For example, the traces of seven memory requests in a RAMCloud *get* operation are shown in Table 1. The first five traces represent memory requests in hash indexing, while the other two represent the data retrieving in log area. First, RAMCloud loads a bucket, which is exactly a cache line, into the cache. It then scans the entries in the bucket sequentially to find an entry with matching

Table 1. Trace example.

No.	Inst. Count	Inst. Addr.	Type	Mem. Addr.	Req. Size
1	15767034	0x473c10	R	0x82cfc300	64
2	15767695	0x473560	R	0x82cfc300	8
3	15767715	0x473560	R	0x82cfc308	8
4	15767735	0x473560	R	0x82cfc310	8
5	15767792	0x47352a	R	0x82cfc310	8
6	15767872	0x4a5a7a	R	0x7099a5c0	64
7	15767876	0x4a5a7a	R	0x7099a600	64

partial hash, as shown in Trace 2–4. After three failed attempts, RAMCloud finds the right hash, unpack the entry, and follow the pointer to retrieve the key-value pair stored in the log area in Trace 5. Finally it fetches the corresponding records in the log, extract the key, and make a comparison with given key as shown in Trace 6–7.

From this example, we can find that it takes more than eight hundred instructions between the access to the hash table and the one to data. Thus, if we can prepare data in advance before data access requests happen, the memory access performance can be improved. In the next section, we will introduce how to achieve this with data prefetching.

3   Prefetching Architecture Design

In this section, we first provide an overview of prefetching architecture proposed in this work. Then, the key components employed in this architecture are introduced in details.

3.1   Structure Overview

A computer system running IMKV is illustrated in Fig. 3. Note that other cache levels other than last level cache (LLC) are hidden to save space. As shown in Fig. 3, in order to enable dedicated prefetching mechanisms in IMKV, several extra components are added into the memory controller. These components include "index range registers" (IRRs), a "prefetching address control unit" (PACU), and a "prefetching size control unit" (PSCU). The basic flow of prefetching is described in details as follows.

As shown in Fig. 4, while a memory request is processed to access memory (step 1), it is sent to IRR at the same time (step 2). The purpose of IRRs is to detect whether the memory request is accessing the hash index or not. If the request is accessing index, a data prefetching process is triggered. The index data retrieved from memory are sent to PACU to detect the addresses to prefetch data (step 3). Then, these addresses are sent to PSCU to identify the

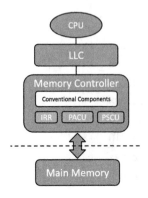

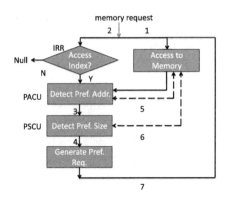

Fig. 3. Architecture overview.

Fig. 4. Memory access flow with prefetching.

size of data to be prefetched (step 4). Note that both PACU and PSCU may also access memory based on the mechanisms adopted in them (steps 5 and 6). With information of prefetching addresses and sizes, the corresponding prefetching requests are generated (step 7). Note that one or multiple prefetching requests may be generated based on output from PACU and PSCU.

Apparently, the efficiency and design overhead of prefetching depends on design of these components. In following subsections, design details of these components will be introduced. Especially, for PSCU and PACU, different architectures are explored.

3.2 Index Range Register (IRR)

As mentioned before, we rely on IRRs to determine whether a memory request is trying to access the hash table of an IMKV so that a proper prefetching is triggered. This modification to memory controller is feasible. In fact memory controllers provide sets of software accessible registers [23]. Since the hash table usually accommodates a contiguous range of virtual addresses, we need two programmable Index Range Registers (IRRs) to keep the start and end address of the hash table. Note that we assume that all memory resource with a memory controller is allocated to one IMKV. Thus, only one set of IRRs are needed.

We address that one obstacle of using IRR is that physical addresses instead of virtual addresses of memory requests are sent to the memory controller for response. One possible solution is to modify hardware to send both physical and virtual addresses to memory controller. However, the design overhead is non-trivial. Instead, we modify the kernel library of memory allocation to ensure that a contiguous range of physical addresses is allocated to hash table during initialization of an IMKV.

We design a set of system calls that allow applications to change the value of IRRs. Currently we have modified applications by hand to insert the system calls to set the lower/upper bound when the IMKV requests memory allocation for the hash table. Note that this process can be automated by compiler in the future. With the help of IRRs, all memory requests whose addresses are in the hash table range are forwarded to the PACU, which is introduced in the next subsection.

3.3 Prefetching Address Control Unit (PACU)

With the help of IRR, each access to the index of IMKV has potential to trigger a data prefetching to speed up the following request of value retrieval. In order to achieve efficient data prefetching, the first critical design issue is to find out the starting address of value data from index information. However, this process is not straightforward. For example, in RAMCloud, each hash bucket has eight index entries. It means that, there are eight prospective addresses of value data in a single bucket.

Naive Exhausted Prefetching. One simple solution is to prepare all potential value data within the same hash bucket before the address of correct value is computed. For example, in RAMCloud, all value data indexed by valid entries in the same bucket are prefetched. Although these indexes are located in the same bucket, the data may be distributed in different ranks or banks. Thus, it is possible to leverage the parallelism of main memory.

This method works efficiently when the index utilization is low. In other words, if there are too many valid entries in a bucket, we may not gain any benefits from data prefetching. The reason can be explained in two-folds. First, due to limited memory rank and bank numbers, the more values we prefetch at the same time, the higher probability they may conflict during prefetching. Thus, the efficiency decreases as the utilization of index memory increases. Second, prefetching too many data at the same time will also impact other memory accesses. In Sect. 4, we will demonstrate that this simple method cannot work well when the average utilization is more than 50 %.

In order to identify proper value to be prefetched rather than prefetching all of them, we further propose two types of techniques in this work: *in-situ index processing* and *value address prediction*.

In-situ Index Processing. In-situ index processing architecture is extended from the accelerator design called Widx [10]. The basic idea is to processing hash index lookup inside memory controller with dedicated hardware design. Then, the corresponded data is prefetched. Similar to Widx, dedicated processing logic are required to perform hash index lookup. However, the Widx architecture needs to be substantially modified when being adopted in our design. It is mainly because Widx is proposed as a co-processor for relational DBMS, which is different from our target, in-memory KV store, in this work.

First, since the prefetching is simply triggered by accessing hash table, the accelerator for hash index lookup is not explicitly controlled by IMKV. In addition, the extra overhead for communication between CPU and accelerator is significantly reduced. However, we need a dedicated RAM in memory controller to store the instructions for processing hash function. Second, Widx only works with linked-list style hash index structure. Thus, modification is needed to make our design work with bucket data structure like that in RAMCloud. The advantage of RAM is that in-situ index processing can be extended to work with different hash index structure through uploading dedicated instructions. Third, different with Widx, which only returns index lookup result to processor, our design needs to issue memory prefetching requests based on the lookup result.

Value Address Prediction. Obviously, in-situ index processing can always find out the correct address to prefetch data. However, its major drawback is that substantial design overhead may be induced due to several reasons. First, since the original key is normally required in memory controller for further index processing, extra hardware support is required. In addition, software level modification is needed to identify the key to be forwarded. Second, the design overhead inside memory controller for index processing (e.g. hash function) is non-trivial. In order to overcome this limitation, we further propose alternative techniques based on prediction.

The prediction technique is to leverage the temporal locality in data access patterns. In other words, for data indexed in the same hash bucket, one of them may be accessed repeatedly during a period. For such access patterns with good temporal locality, there is high possibility that the entry containing correct data addressed in the last access will be accessed again. Thus, it is beneficial to prefetch data indexed by this entry.

The key issue of prediction is to indicate the entry containing correct address in the last data retrieval. We propose to design additional hit table in hardware to record the hit history of these index entries. One critical issue is to decide the size of hit table. For example, in RAMCloud, a 2 GByte hash table requires a 12 MByte hit table to fully record hit history of all hash entries. To fully integrate such size hit table in memory controller is not feasible due to both area and scalability issues. Like Centaur [24], we design hit table in a memory buffer between memory controller and main memory, rather than in memory controller or main memory. The hit table shares the same index from key hashing. PACU can acquire hit table entry off-chip when it is triggered by IRRs. Advantages to implement hit table in memory buffer is faster access than in main memory and better scalability than fixed size in memory controller. In case that we have to consider overhead of hit table to reduce its size at huge hash table, it is possible that it cannot fully cover all hashing entries. In such cases, if the key hashing index is out of the range of hit table, a default prediction scheme of loading the first entry in the hash bucket can be employed. In Sect. 4, we evaluate hit table in constant latency, and also maximum size to cover whole hash table. The other critical issue is how to update hit table. Through modification of *get* operation, we propose IMKVs to update hit table every time when data retrieving finish. By this way, hit table contains latest access entries in hash table. Although interferences from different threads and bad temporal or spatial locality in data retrieving reduce predication accuracy, as show in Sect. 4, we will demonstrate that this simple method still works well when accuracy is as low as 20 %. Especially, the fact that accuracy of predication is increased as hash table utilization is decreased opens a door for IMKVs to control accuracy in need.

3.4   Prefetching Size Control Unit (PSCU)

With the help of PACU, we can decide where to prefetch data. Then, the next critical issue is to determine how many data we should prefetch from main memory. As shown in Fig. 3, we rely on the component called prefetching size control unit (PSCU) in this work. There are two corresponding choices for design of PSCU, which are introduced in the following two paragraphs. Although the determination of prefetching size is orthogonal to the design of PACU, these two components affect each other on the efficiency of prefetching.

Run-Time Size Determination. Similar to in-situ index processing, we can leverage the accelerator in memory controller to detect the prefetching size based on the data stored at prefetching address. In other words, we employ dedicated logic to obtain the size of value dynamically. This method is feasible because the size of a value is normally stored together with value data in KV store. For example, the first several bytes of value data in RAMCloud contains the size information. Obviously, if in-situ processing accelerator is employed in PACU, the hardware can be shared with PSCU to accurately determine prefetching address and prefetching size.

Average Size Profiling. When the naive prefetching or the address prediction technique is employed, it is not efficient to add an accelerator just for determination of prefetching size. Thus, a profiling based technique is preferred for in these two cases.

- *Static Profiling.* A simple but efficient method is to perform static profiling in advance to calculate the average value size. This static method is preferred when the size of values do not vary a lot.
- *Dynamic Profiling.* An alternative is to determine the run-time average value dynamically. This method is more efficient than static one when the value sizes vary significantly. However, it requires extra support to record the history of value size. In order to reduce hardware overhead, we propose software method profiles past accessed size of KVs and update PSCU periodically.

Both static and dynamic profiling methods are based on facts that in parts of IMKVs application, such as financial services, KV-pair's size does not show big variations. When the prefetching size does not match the value size, the efficiency of prefetching is decreased. If the size of prefetched data is smaller than the real value size, supplementary memory request from CPU is needed to fetch the rest of value data. On the contrary, if the prefetching size is larger than the real value size, memory bandwidth is wasted and other normal memory requests may be affected.

4   Evaluation

In this section, we first introduce the setup for experiments. Then, we provide comprehensive results and analysis. In addition, the design overhead is discussed.

4.1   Experiment Setup

We conduct the experiment on customized trace-driven cycle-accurate simulator, which supports a full CMP architecture, including out-of-order multi-issue multi-processors, two-level cache hierarchy, shared-cache coherent protocol, 2-D mesh NOC, main memory controller and DRAM device. Be specific, CPU, cache hierarchy and NOC are modeled by home-made simulator, while the memory controller and DRAM device are modeled by DRAMSim2 [21], and power is evaluated on DRAM device. Performance is evaluated by average memory request latency. The detailed configuration of the experiment and parameters used in simulation are shown in Table 2.

Table 2. Detailed configuration of experiment platform

Unit	Configurations
CPU	8 Intel cores, 4 GHz, 128 instruction windows, 4issue/4commit (one memory op) per cycle, 16 MSHR
L1	Private 16 KB 4-way set associative, 64 B line, LRU, R/W 1/ 1-cycle
L2	Shared 4 MB 16-way set associative, 64 B line, LRU,
Cache-coherent	Directory based cache-coherent protocol: MESI
NOC	2×4 mesh NOC, one router per node, x-y direction based routing, 8 flits per data packet, 1 flit per control packet
Memory controller	2 memory controllers, 16 GB, 32 entries transaction queue,
	32-entry command queue, FR-FCFS scheduling, open page policy, rank-interleave address mapping
DRAM device	Micron DDR3-1333 Mhz, x8, 8Banks, 32768 Rows/Bank, 1024 Columns/Row, 1 KB page size, BL = 8

The benchmarks are run on RAMCloud [22], which is a widely-adopted multithread IMKV application. We use typical IMKV requests (128 B, 256 B and 512 B value size) from YCSB [6] benchmark to drive KV operations in RAMCloud. To setup initial database in RAMCloud, we generate sufficient KV pairs to initialize RAMCloud's memory, in total 1 GB segmented log and 100 MB hash table. Based on execution of RAMCloud, we collect traces of multithreaded KV operations on real CMP machine and feed traces to simulator. During simulation, we execute 10 billion instructions of KV benchmarks for rapid estimation. Table 3 shows 12 typical mixed workloads of KV operations in IMKV requests, which have an increasing size of average value size in Byte.

4.2   Experiment Results

In order to address the impact of each design factor related to design of PACU and PSCU, the synthetic workloads are first simulated. Then, the evaluation using real workloads is discussed. Note that we use normalized average "memory request latency" as the metric of memory access performance.

Synthetic Workloads Results. In Fig. 5, the impact of prefetching size on performance is evaluated. There are three sets of workloads, in each of which the value size is fixed. Assume that the static profiling method is employed. The prefetching size varies from 128 B to 1024 B to demonstrate its impact. In this experiment, the correct prefetching address is always provided to isolate the effect of PACU. For comparison, the baseline without using any prefetching is also presented and all results are normalized to it.

As shown in the Fig. 5(a), the best performance is achieved when the prefetching size matches the value size. In addition, we can observe that the efficiency of prefetching increases with value size. When the prefetching size is smaller than the value size, the efficiency of prefetching decreases. But, we can find that performance is still improved compared to the baseline. It is because part of value data is prefetched and the rest is requested by CPU through normal access. The results also show that prefetching efficiency is reduced when more data than value are prefetched. It is because its effect on memory bandwidth and other normal requests has offsets its benefits from data prefetching.

In Fig. 5(b), the efficiency of naive exhausted prefetching is evaluated. Similar to last experiment, there are three sets of workloads with fixed value size. In order to isolate the effect of prefetching size, we assume that prefetching size always matches the value size. For each workload, we vary the average hash bucket utilization through software level control, so that prefetching size by naive exhausted method varies from 2 KVs to 8 KVs. Besides the baseline, we also present one set of result using in-situ hash processing when utilization is 4 KVs per hash index. Here, we skip 1 KV case, because hash table utilization is too low, and exhausted method always prefetch correct data as in-situ method. From the results we can tell that the efficiency of naive exhausted prefetching decreases as the utilization of bucket increases. Normally, we cannot gain any

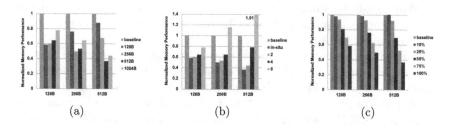

Fig. 5. (a) Effect of prefetching size. (b) Efficiency of naive exhausted prefetching. (c) Effect of prefetching accuracy.

Table 3. Detailed configuration of workloads

Workloads	128B-R	128B-W	256B-R	256B-W	512B-R	512B-W	Avg(Byte)
mix1	96.7%	0.8%	1.5%	0.1%	0.6%	0.5%	134.1
mix2	70.0%	9.5%	7.4%	2.4%	8.2%	2.7%	182.3
mix3	34.1%	34.0%	10.4%	5.5%	10.3%	5.7%	210.1
mix4	37.2%	19.3%	24.4%	5.1%	8.7%	5.3%	219.5
mix5	13.4%	10.5%	61.6%	12.5%	1.5%	0.5%	230.5
mix6	15.0%	10.0%	37.5%	27.5%	7.5%	2.5%	249.6
mix7	17.4%	6.6%	38.2%	15.6%	15.2%	7.1%	282.5
mix8	8.0%	5.0%	32.5%	22.5%	27.0%	5.0%	321.3
mix9	17.1%	5.1%	13.1%	5.0%	58.6%	1.3%	380.8
mix10	7.5%	2.5%	15.0%	10.0%	37.5%	27.5%	409.6
mix11	5.7%	1.1%	19.8%	7.7%	54.8%	11.2%	416.1
mix12	6.4%	5.2%	7.3%	6.8%	37.8%	36.8%	432.0

benefits when the utilization is higher than 50%. In addition, we can tell that its impact on performance increases with the value size.

In Fig. 5(c), the efficiency of address prediction is evaluated, in respect of prediction accuracy. In this experiment, we assume that the value size is fixed and is known in advance for each workload. Thus, the performance is only affected by the prefetching address prediction. For each workload, we vary the prediction accuracy from 10% to 100%. Note that the case of 100% accurate reflects the result when the in-situ hash processing is employed. We can find that performance is improved by more than 20% for all workloads when the prediction accuracy is higher than 50%. In worse case, 20% predication accuracy still achieves about 10% improvement. The reason is the temporal locality in IMKVs is different from scientific applications, thus the replacement of cache line by prefetched data doesn't impact much on miss rate of last level cache. It proves the feasibility of prefetching address prediction in PACU, such as hit table method, especially for large value size.

Real Workloads Results. In this section, we present performance simulation results based on real workloads listed in Table 3. In addition, the energy overhead caused by prefetching is also included.

We repeat an experiment similar to that in Fig. 5(a), in which different prefetching sizes are applied with real workloads. Normalized performance results are shown in Fig. 6. Besides the baseline without using prefetching, the in-situ case using in-situ processing for both prefetching address and size is also compared in the Fig. 6. We can find that the efficiency of prefetching relies on proper prefetching size. In-situ case gains best performance due to accuracy. The second optimized prefetching sizes found in the figure for different workloads are closed

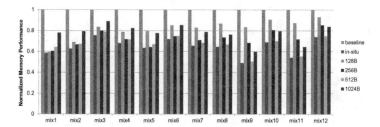

Fig. 6. Effect of prefetching size with real workloads.

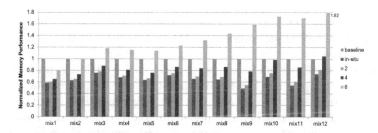

Fig. 7. Efficiency of naive exhausted prefetching with real workloads.

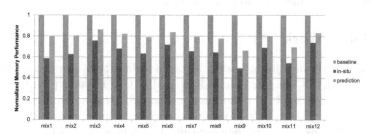

Fig. 8. In-situ processing vs. prediction.

to the average value sizes calculated in Table 3. It proves average size profiling method can achieve improvements on performance.

In Fig. 7, the naive exhausted prefetching with in-situ method is applied with real workloads. We can draw the similar conclusion that it only works when the bucket utilization is lower than 50 %, and its offsets impact on performance increases with the average value size. Basically, it is hard for hash table with full utilization of buckets to gain benefits through naive exhausted prfetching.

In Fig. 8, we compare the in-situ case with best performance to case with lowest design overhead. As mentioned before, the in-situ case is to use in-situ processing for both prefetching address and size with most accuracy. The case with lowest overhead is to use dynamic profiling and the prefetching address prediction (e.g. hit table method). Experiment shows hit table method can achieve about 50 % accuracy of address predication on average. We find that the prefetch-

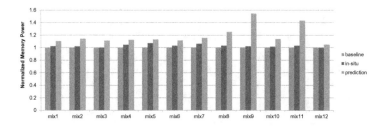

Fig. 9. Extra power consumption.

ing based on simple profiling and prediction can also improve performance. On average, performance is improved by 35.4 % in in-situ case and is improved by 21 % in the latter case.

Although prefetching can help improve performance of IMKV, it also induces extra power consumption. In Fig. 9, we demonstrate the normalized power results for different workloads. We can find that the power overhead is trivial for in-situ prefetching case. It is because prefetching only changes the sequence of load data value without inducing extra memory requests. However, with the prediction based prefetching, the power consumption is not always negligible due to incorrect prediction and dynamic profiling.

5   Related Work

Most in-memory stores using hash table as indexing structure: Memcached [2, 18], Redis [3], RAMCloud [22], MemC3 [8], and MICA [15] all exploit hashing to achieve low latency and high performance. Standard Memcached uses a classical hash table design to index the key-value entries, with linked-list-based chaining to handle collisions. Its cache replacement algorithm is strict LRU, also based on linked lists. RAMCloud [22] employs a cache-optimized hash table layout to minimize the memory cache misses. MemC3 [8] is optimized for read-mostly workload by applying CLOCK-based eviction algorithm and concurrent optimistic cuckoo hashing. MICA [15] enables parallel access to partitioned data, utilizes lossy concurrent hash indexes, and bulk chaining techniques to handle both read- and write-intensive workloads. These mechanisms could be layered on top of our data prefetching schemes to achieve the same goals.

Prefetching is a commonly used method to hide the increasing latency of accesses to main memory. Various studies have been conducted to investigate the benefits of prefetching. These techniques can be classified as software-controlled or hardware-controlled. Software-controlled prefetching techniques [19,26] use special prefetch instructions to asynchronously pre-load cache blocks. Additional instructions must be inserted and executed in the applications. Unlike software-controlled method, hardware-controlled prefetching techniques [12] construct pre-fetcher triggered by dedicated conditions to retrieve data in advance. PADC [12] estimates the usefulness of prefetch requests, adaptively prioritize between demand and prefetch requests, and drop useless prefetches. Lee et al. [13] study the DRAM bank-level parallelism issues in the presence of prefetching. Based on commercial microprocessors equipped with data prefetch engines [23], [9] evaluate accurate measurement of performance metrics through adaptive prefetching scheme depending workloads natures. According to location of prefetching initiator, memory-side prefetching [27], in tandem with processor-side prefetcher to leverage knowledge of DRAM state, answers what/when/where to prefetch. In contracts, our work focuses on hash table prefetching in IMKVS and therefore has the application-specific knowledge of regular access pattern in workloads to improve memory access performance.

Co-processor has been widely used for acceleration of specific applications. Recently, for hashing index based IMKV, Babak et al. propose Widx [10], an on-chip accelerator for database hash index lookups. Widx uses a custom RISC core to achieve high-performance hashing computation. Widx walks multiple hash buckets concurrently to exploit the inter-key parallelism. We extend Widx in memory controller as in-situ method to cover not only linked-list style, but also bucket style hash index structure, to issue accurate prefetching requests to improve data retrieving based on hash lookup result.

6   Conclusion

In-memory KV stores have been extensively employed for modern applications for high performance data retrieval. Since hashing based index is widely adopted in these KV stores, the memory access patterns for data retrieval are regular. Thus, data prefetching technique can be employed to improve performance of memory access. In this work, with detailed analysis of data access pattern in real IMKVs, we propose several practical prefetching techniques. The in-situ processing based prefetching can achieve the best performance but also induces most overhead. The prediction and profiling based prefetching can also improve performance with moderate design overhead. However, it may induce non-trivial power overhead. Considering the trade-off, proper prefetching should be adopted in real cases for different design goals.

Acknowledgements. This work was partially supported by National High-tech R&D Program of China (2013AA013201) and in part by National Natural Science Foundation of China (61202072, 61272132, 61221062).

References

1. Intel 64 and IA-32 Architectures Software Developers Manuals. www.intel.com/products/processor/manuals
2. Memcached. http://memcached.org/
3. Redis. http://redis.io/
4. Cattell, R.: Scalable SQLA and NoSQL data stores. SIGMOD Rec. **39**(4), 12–27 (2011)

5. Chang, F., Dean, J., Ghemawat, S., Hsieh, W.C., Wallach, D.A., Burrows, M., Chandra, T., Fikes, A., Gruber, R.E.: Bigtable: a distributed storage system for structured data. ACM Trans. Comput. Syst. **26**(2), 4:1–4:26 (2008)

6. Cooper, B.F., Silberstein, A., Tam, E., Ramakrishnan, R., Sears, R.: Benchmarking cloud serving systems with YCSB. In: Proceedings of the 1st ACM Symposium on Cloud Computing, pp. 143–154. ACM (2010)

7. DeCandia, G., Hastorun, D., Jampani, M., Kakulapati, G., Lakshman, A., Pilchin, A., Sivasubramanian, S., Vosshall, P., Vogels, W.: Dynamo: Amazon's highly available key-value store. In: Proceedings of the 21st ACM Symposium on Operating Systems Principles, SOSP 2007, pp. 205–220. ACM, New York (2007)

8. Fan, B., Andersen, D.G., Kaminsky, M.: MemC3: compact and concurrent memcache with dumber caching and smarter hashing. In: Proceedings of the 10th USENIX Conference on Networked Systems Design and Implementation, NSDI 2013, pp. 371–384. USENIX Association, Berkeley (2013)

9. Jiménez, V., Cazorla, F.J., Gioiosa, R., Buyuktosunoglu, A., Bose, P., O'Connell, F.P., Mealey, B.G.: Adaptive prefetching on POWER7: improving performance and power consumption. ACM Trans. Parallel Comput. **1**(1), 4:1–4:25 (2014)

10. Kocberber, O., Grot, B., Picorel, J., Falsafi, B., Lim, K., Ranganathan, P.: Meet the walkers: accelerating index traversals for in-memory databases. In: Proceedings of the 46th Annual IEEE/ACM International Symposium on Microarchitecture, MICRO 46, pp. 468–479. ACM, New York (2013)

11. Lakshman, A., Malik, P.: Cassandra: a decentralized structured storage system. SIGOPS Oper. Syst. Rev. **44**(2), 35–40 (2010)

12. Lee, C.J., Mutlu, O., Narasiman, V., Patt, Y.N.: Prefetch-aware DRAM controllers. In: Proceedings of the 41st Annual IEEE/ACM International Symposium on Microarchitecture, MICRO 41, pp. 200–209. IEEE Computer Society, Washington, DC (2008)

13. Lee, C.J., Narasiman, V., Mutlu, O., Patt, Y.N.: Improving memory bank-level parallelism in the presence of prefetching. In: Proceedings of the 42nd Annual IEEE/ACM International Symposium on Microarchitecture, MICRO 42, pp. 327–336. ACM, New York (2009)

14. Liao, S.w., Hung, T.H., Nguyen, D., Chou, C., Tu, C., Zhou, H.: Machine learning-based prefetch optimization for data center applications. In: Proceedings of the Conference on High Performance Computing Networking, Storage and Analysis, SC 2009, pp. 56:1–56:10. ACM, New York (2009)

15. Lim, H., Han, D., Andersen, D.G., Kaminsky, M.: MICA: a holistic approach to fast in-memory key-value storage. In: 11th USENIX Symposium on Networked Systems Design and Implementation, NSDI 2014, pp. 429–444. USENIX Association, Seattle (2014)

16. Loos, P.D.P., Lechtenbrger, J., Vossen, G., Zeier, A., Krger, J., Mller, J., Lehner, W., Kossmann, D., Fabian, B., Gnther, O., Winter, R.: In-memory databases in business information systems. Bus. Inf. Syst. Eng. **3**(6), 389–395 (2011)

17. Luk, C.K., Cohn, R., Muth, R., Patil, H., Klauser, A., Lowney, G., Wallace, S., Reddi, V.J., Hazelwood, K.: Pin: building customized program analysis tools with dynamic instrumentation. In: ACM Sigplan Notices, vol. 40, pp. 190–200. ACM (2005)

18. Nishtala, R., Fugal, H., Grimm, S., Kwiatkowski, M., Lee, H., Li, H.C., McElroy, R., Paleczny, M., Peek, D., Saab, P., Stafford, D., Tung, T., Venkataramani, V.: Scaling memcache at Facebook. In: Presented as part of the 10th USENIX Symposium on Networked Systems Design and Implementation, NSDI 2013, pp. 385–398. USENIX, Lombard (2013)

19. Ortega, D., Ayguadé, E., Baer, J.L., Valero, M.: Cost-effective compiler directed memory prefetching and bypassing. In: Proceedings of the 2002 International Conference on Parallel Architectures and Compilation Techniques, PACT 2002, pp. 189–198. IEEE Computer Society, Washington, DC (2002)

20. Plattner, H., Zeier, A.: In-memory Data Management: Technology and Applications. Springer Science & Business Media, Heidelberg (2012)

21. Rosenfeld, P., Cooper-Balis, E., Jacob, B.: DRAMSim2: a cycle accurate memory system simulator. Comput. Archit. Lett. **10**(1), 16–19 (2011)

22. Rumble, S.M., Kejriwal, A., Ousterhout, J.K.: Log-structured memory for DRAM-based storage. In: Schroeder, B., Thereska, E. (eds.) Proceedings of the 12th USENIX Conference on File and Storage Technologies, FAST 2014, Santa Clara, CA, USA, 17–20 February 2014. pp. 1–16. USENIX (2014)

23. Sinharoy, B., Kalla, R., Starke, W.J., Le, H.Q., Cargnoni, R., Van Norstrand, J.A., Ronchetti, B.J., Stuecheli, J., Leenstra, J., Guthrie, G.L., Nguyen, D.Q., Blaner, B., Marino, C.F., Retter, E., Williams, P.: IBM POWER7 multicore server processor. IBM J. Res. Dev. **55**(3), 1:1–1:29 (2011)

24. Stuecheli, J.: Next Generation POWER microprocessor. http://www.hotchips.org/archives/2010s/hc25/

25. Wu, C.J., Jaleel, A., Martonosi, M., Steely, Jr., S.C., Emer, J.: PACMan: prefetch-aware cache management for high performance caching. In: Proceedings of the 44th Annual IEEE/ACM International Symposium on Microarchitecture, MICRO 44, pp. 442–453. ACM, New York (2011)

26. Wu, Y.: Efficient discovery of regular stride patterns in irregular programs and its use in compiler prefetching. In: Proceedings of the ACM SIGPLAN 2002 Conference on Programming Language Design and Implementation, PLDI 2002, pp. 210–221. ACM, New York (2002)

27. Yedlapalli, P., Kotra, J., Kultursay, E., Kandemir, M., Das, C.R., Sivasubramaniam, A.: Meeting midway: improving CMP performance with memory-side prefetching. In: Proceedings of the 22nd International Conference on Parallel Architectures and Compilation Techniques, PACT 2013, pp. 289–298. IEEE Press, Piscataway (2013)

28. Zhao, C., Mei, K., Zheng, N.: Design of write merging and read prefetching buffer in DRAM controller for embedded processor. Microprocess. Microsyst. **38**(5), 451–457 (2014)

DDC: Distributed Data Collection Framework for Failure Prediction in Tianhe Supercomputers

Wei Hu[1,2], Yanhuang Jiang[1(✉)], Guangming Liu[1,2], Wenrui Dong[1,2], and Guilin Cai[1]

[1] College of Computer, National University of Defense Technology, Changsha, China
w-hu@qq.com, yhjiang@nudt.edu.cn,
{liugm,dongwr}@nscc-tj.gov.cn, cc_cai@163.com
[2] National Supercomputer Centre of Tianjin, Tianjin, China

Abstract. Reliability has become an issue to the Tianhe supercomputer series with the scaling of the system. Proactive fault-tolerance based on failure prediction turns into an effective way to improve the system's fault tolerance ability. Data collection is the basis of the failure prediction which has a great impact on the prediction accuracy, while current data collection methods for failure prediction only got limited data with large overhead. This paper presents DDC data collection framework for failure prediction in Tianhe supercomputers. DDC adopts a distributed data collection architecture which can fully collect the data related to the compute nodes' health with high efficiency. Through the testing for DDC which ran on TH-1A, the results indicated that DDC had the advantage of low cost and good scalability.

Keywords: Supercomputer · Failure prediction · Data collection method

1 Introduction

Reliability wall has been one of the main obstacles to the roadmap of supercomputers toward Exascale [1]. Supercomputers typically have hundreds of thousands of components, for example, Tianhe-2 supercomputer has 16,000 compute nodes, meaning a total of 3.12 million compute cores. With the amount of components increasing quickly, the MTBF (Mean Time Between Failure) of the system decreases from days to hours [2]. Therefore, for long-running parallel applications it becomes difficult or impossible to complete without confronting failures on supercomputers. MPI (Message Passing Interface) which is the main parallel pattern of scientific applications uses message passing mechanism which could cause the entire application failure as long as one process failing, and this is becoming a major performance impediment for supercomputers due to the work loss.

Checkpoint/Restart(CPR), a typical passive fault-tolerance technology, is currently the most common fault-tolerance method which periodically stores all the compute nodes status and recovers from the failure through the rollback approach after the

© Springer International Publishing Switzerland 2015
Y. Chen et al. (Eds.): APPT 2015, LNCS 9231, pp. 18–32, 2015.
DOI: 10.1007/978-3-319-23216-4_2

failure's occurrence [3, 4]. However, owing to the shorter MTBF and mismatched I/O performance compared to the larger scale of supercomputer computing systems, the significant performance loss of CPR is non-trivial, and this may cause new performance problem with larger systems toward exscale computing.

Proactive fault-tolerance technology which can predict the system failure using prediction model and take protection measures with low overheads in advance is now becoming a new research hotspot. Prediction model is the key of the proactive fault-tolerance technology, meanwhile the prediction accuracy determines the availability of the whole proactive fault-tolerance system. The prediction model based on data driven is suitable for large-scale systems and has good accuracy. So the fundamental problem is to obtain the system status data related to failure which are used for the prediction model.

To deal with the problem which MTBF decreasing rapidly in Tianhe supercomputers, we are trying to establish a ·proactive fault-tolerance system in which data collection for failure prediction is an important part. This paper presents a Distributed Data Collection Framework (DDC) to solve the data collection problems in large-scale systems. The paper is structured as follows. Related work is provided in Sect. 2. Section 3 presents the multiple data sources combined prediction model and the DDC design in Tianhe-1A. Section 4 gives the evaluation of DDC and Sect. 5 draws the conclusions and outlines our future work.

2 Related Work

Currently the data which the failure prediction model uses fall into two types: one is the RAS-based (Reliability, Availability, and Serviceability) log data which the supercomputer monitor system provides; the other is the compute node hardware status data and running status data.

RAS log data collected by the monitor system are the records of the RAS related events that occur across the machine. These data include hard errors, soft errors, software problems and machine checks. The researchers of Rutgers University and IBM company [5–7], Lan research team [8–10], Oliner research team [11–13] and some other researchers [14–17] built failure prediction model based on RAS log data. RAS data which record the system hardware and software events have two flaws: firstly, RAS data are incomplete due to the event logging mechanism which cannot record the full-time status variation of the hardware and software, and this may lead to false negatives. Secondly, owning to the complexity of the system, the definitions of log events cannot be completely accurate which are easy to produce false positives. Based on the above reasons, the accuracy of the failure prediction model based on RAS data is limited due to the characteristics of the RAS data themselves.

The compute node hardware status data include hardware temperature, voltage, fan and power related status data. Scott [18], Nagarajan [19] and Rajachandrasekar [20] did the research on the failure prediction model using the hardware status data through IPMI (Intelligent Platform Management Interface). The compute node running status data typically refer to the CPU, memory, network and I/O-related status data, such as CPU load, memory usage, network statistics, I/O bandwidth and so on. Since most compute nodes of supercomputer are isomorphic on which running are the similar scientific applications, so the data obtained from the compute node operating system may reflect the health status of the nodes. Sahoo [11] proposed failure prediction model using data sets consisted of log records and the compute node running status data. The research of failure prediction model using the compute node running status data is not so much due to the difficulties on data collection. Existing cluster monitor tools like PARMON [21], Ganglia [22] and Ovis-2 [23] have the function of data collection which cannot meet the actual needs owing to the small number of data attributes, nontrivial collection overheads.

From the present research it is easy to find that the data used for failure prediction for supercomputers have the following characteristics which are the motivations for the DDC development.

- One-sidedness: The existing data collection methods are mostly committed to collect the data of a particular aspect of the system which cannot accurately reflect the overall status of the target system.
- Discreteness: Data used now for failure prediction are discrete and bursty, which cannot fully record the status of the computing system and significantly affect the prediction accuracy.
- High Overhead: The overheads of data collection mainly consist of three parts, CPU overhead, network overhead and storage overhead. CPU overhead can be ignored due to the little CPU overhead itself versus to more powerful CPU performance. But with the increasing scale of the supercomputer, network overhead and storage overhead are the true blocks to the data collection.

3 The DDC Design

3.1 Tianhe Supercomputer Series

DDC was designed for Tianhe supercomputer series which were developed by National University of Defense Technology. This series of supercomputers including Tianhe-1, Tianhe-1A and Tianhe-2, are typical MPP (Massive Parallel Processing) systems which have the same features as follows.

- Using accelerator/co-processor technology. Tianhe-2 is using Intel Xeon Phi processors to speed up computation while Tianhe-1A, upgraded from Tianhe-1, is using NVIDIA GPUs to accelerate computation.
- Proprietary high-speed interconnection network. Tianhe supercomputer series adopt high-radix Network Routing Chips (NRC) and high-speed Network Interface Chips (NIC) to implement proprietary network protocol based on fat-tree topology.
- Parallel file system based on Lustre. Tianhe-1A uses the Lustre file system as the parallel file system while Tianhe-2 adopts H2IO(Hybrid and Hierarchy I/O stack) based on Lustre and I/O nodes.
- Monitor system based on dedicated Ethernet.

DDC applies to all Tianhe supercomputers which have the similar architecture. This paper describes DDC in Tianhe-1A supercomputer which can also run in Tianhe-2 by parameter configurations. Figure 1 shows the Tianhe-1A architecture in detail. There are 140 cabinets in Tianhe-1A, including 112 compute cabinets, 8 service cabinets, 6 communication cabinets, and 14 I/O cabinets. Each compute cabinet contains 4 compute frames and each frame contains 16 compute nodes.

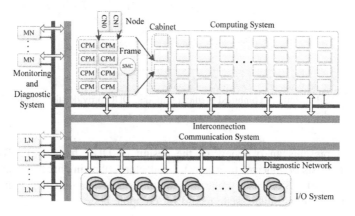

Fig. 1. Tianhe-1A architecture

3.2 Multiple Data Sources Combined Prediction Model

The failure prediction model which is the key of the whole proactive fault-tolerance system has obstacles in acquiring the valid data related to the health status of the compute nodes, and this can be solved by the DDC framework.

Based on the architecture of the Tianhe supercomputer series, this paper presents the multiple data sources combined prediction model as the Fig. 2 shows. This prediction model has two tiers. The first tier includes two different real-time prediction models which provide real-time failure prediction respectively. The second tier provides the intelligent prediction model based on the results from the first tier in order to give the optimal prediction results. All these models are based on the data collected from the system as the figure denotes. This paper focuses on the data collection method for failure prediction, the prediction models will be detailed in another paper.

3.3 An Overview of the DDC Design

Data collection which is the foundation of the entire procedure of failure prediction has two functions: The first is to provide data set for the training of prediction model, where the training data set includes not only the initial training set in the establishment phase of prediction model but also the incremental data set in the upgrade phase of prediction model. The second is to provide real-time data to prediction model for real-time failure prediction.

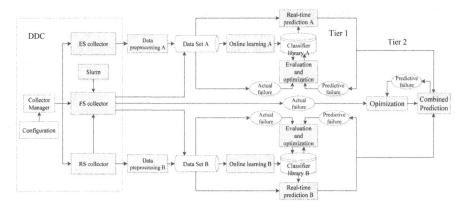

Fig. 2. Multiple data sources combined prediction model. DDC provides the data for the failure prediction model

Figure 3 presents an overview of the design of DDC framework. The DDC framework consists of collector manager, ES collector (collecting hardware status data for compute node), RS collector (collecting running status data for compute node) and FS collector (collecting failure state record for compute node).

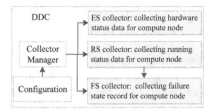

Fig. 3. An overview of DDC framework. Besides configuration files DDC incorporates four units, collector manager, ES collector, RS collector and FS collector

Collector Manager. Collector manager is used to control the operation of the entire data collection system whose main functions are as follows:

- Basic control and configuration. Collector manager is used to start or end the data collection, and configure operating parameters, such as data collection characteristics, collection time interval, data store path and so on.
- Monitoring the operating state of each data collection module. Collector manager periodically checks the logs of each data collection module to handle exception and keep the modules running normally.

ES Collector. ES collector is used to collect and record the hardware status data for compute node. These data mainly denote hardware status related to compute node which reflect the real-time physical status of the hardware components such as temperature, voltage, current, fan speed and so on.

There is a dedicated Ethernet in the monitor system of Tianhe-1A which used for system control and maintenance, whose central hardware is SMC (System Management Controller). Each compute cabinet of Tianhe-1A is comprised of 4 frames, and each frame which includes 16 compute nodes is equipped with one SMC as shown in Fig. 1. SMC is not only responsible for internal monitoring of a frame but also provide external access interface by using a fixed IP address.

ES collector is designed to collect the compute node hardware status data through SMC in parallel using multiple threads based on dedicated Ethernet. As the Fig. 4 shows, ES collector has the following characteristics: firstly, it is efficient to collect all the 16 compute nodes data through once access to the corresponding SMC using client-server method. Secondly, the programming methods of TCP/IP socket and multi-thread optimize the access efficiency, reduce the access overhead and avoid making the manager node become a bottleneck. Thirdly, this method is fast and almost no overhead to the applications running on the compute nodes due to using dedicated Ethernet.

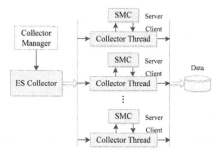

Fig. 4. ES collector collects the hardware status data for compute node using multiple threads based on dedicated Ethernet

RS Collector. RS collector is designed to collect and record the compute node running status data which is related to the system activity commonly referred to as SAR (System Activity Report) data. SAR data are the status data and statistical data of all parts of the system typically including CPU, memory, network, I/O and so on. Commonly compute nodes of supercomputer have the same configuration, therefore the SAR data can effectively reflect the system running status of compute nodes in real time.

With the increasing scale of the supercomputer, it means more overhead to collect much data from more compute nodes through critical path like interconnection and shared storage. Large scales of frequent data transmission and storage operations not only consume the system performance, but also affect the system stability.

To solve this problem, RS collector adopts a distributed data collection architecture which can greatly reduce the amount of data needed to be transmitted and stored. The main considerations are as follows:

- Every compute node has a data collection process which is responsible for data collection, transmission and store.
- All of the compute nodes are divided into groups wherein the nodes probe each other and collect data in the way like a one-way circular linked list. In any group each node not only collects and stores its own data but also sends the data to the next node in the linked list. In other words each node backups the t_b time length data of the previous node and the node itself in the linked list.
- The data set consists of two parts: When a node fails, the next node in the linked list will transmit the backup data to the shared storage as the failure node status data. The normal node status data are stored from the selected normal node according to the configuration which is only a small part of all the normal status data.
- The prediction model based on the compute node running status data is sent to each compute node to perform real-time failure prediction respectively.

Figure 5 shows the distributed architecture of the RS collector with the details related to data collection method, data transmission and storing method. The dashed lines represent the logical relationship of data transmission among the nodes, while the solid line arrows are the actual physical data transmission path.

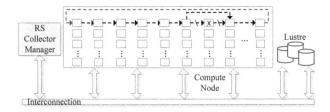

Fig. 5. RS collector collects the compute node running status data using distributed architecture

Data Collection. RS collector gets the running status data effectively through analyzing the/proc file system which is a virtual file system and part of the linux kernel./ proc provides a dynamic interface which can view the running information of the operating system, such as process information, CPU information and so on. In order to improve the efficiency of data collection and analysis, RS collector reads the/proc related files in parallel and then integrates the data to a complete record. The data collection interval of this way can be reduced to milliseconds with little overhead.

By analyzing the files or folders in the /proc of Tianhe-1A compute node such as cpuinfo, slabinfo, uptime, net/, sys/, scsi/ and so on, the selected 136 data attributes which are closely related to the node running status are collected.

Data Storing and Transmission. That is still a small probability event for the compute node failure, so most of the data collected from the compute node are normal status data which don't need to transmit and store. For failure prediction model, a balanced training set consists of approximately equal numbers of normal and failure status records.

RS collector uses a loop-based data storing and transmission method like one-way circular linked list. This method can greatly reduce the network and I/O overhead since it only transmits and stores the running status data of the failed compute node and little data of normal compute node.

RS collector manager is used to configure and monitor the status of the running status data collection including node grouping, joining, leaving and so on.

The compute nodes are divided into several groups wherein nodes are from different cabinets to avoid the same failure event like power outage and so on. Nodes in the same group form a logical loop structure like one-way circular linked list through sorting the nodes by id numbers. Let us use I_{id} to denote the id number of each node, and $I_{initial}$ is the first node of the system. Suppose α is the grouping coefficient, so the N_{Group} (node grouping number) can be divided using the following formula:

$$N_{Group} = (I_{id} - I_{initial})\%\alpha \tag{1}$$

There are a total of 7168 compute nodes in Tianhe-1A supercomputer with initial node id 0. Suppose that the grouping coefficient is 64, so the whole system is divided into 64 groups and each group has 112 nodes when all the nodes are on line. In Tianhe-1A each cabinet contains 4 frames with total 64 compute nodes, so the nodes in each group are not in the same cabinet when the grouping coefficient is 64.

As shown in Fig. 6, the node collects the running status data and stores it in duplicate for one copy locally in memory and another copy to the next node in the loop. When a node fails or shuts down, the FS collector records the event and notifies RS collector. RS collector performs deleting operation to notify the related previous and next node to complete the node deleting operation and failure status data saving operation. Figure 7 shows the procedure of a node receiving the data of the previous node. If receiving data from previous node within the timeout limit, the node stores the data in memory and waits for the next data transmission. If the data reception exceeds the timeout limit, the node will probe the previous node by sending a message. The abnormal signal will be sent to the FS collector or not according to the ACK reply. The state of the abnormal node will be judged by the FS collector. If the node failure is confirmed, the delete operation will be trigged. When a new node is added, RS collector will perform inserting operation to update the relevant group list and insert the node to the data collection loop.

FS Collector. FS collector is used to collect and record the failure state data of compute node through integrating three kinds of data including RS collector alarm data, SLURM (Simple Linux Utility for Resource Management) data and maintenance staffs records.

RS collector alarm data denote to the abnormal signals which have been mentioned in the last section. When one node probe the previous node without the ACK reply, the node will issue the abnormal signal related to the previous node to the RS collector manager. And this record will also be sent to FS collector.

SLURM is an open-source resource manager designed for Linux clusters which provides a framework for starting, executing and monitoring work on a set of allocated nodes. SLURM also records the node state variations including ALLOCATED,

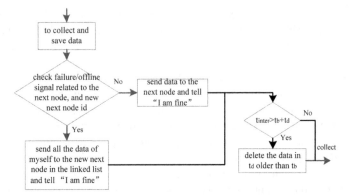

Fig. 6. The flow chart of collecting and transmitting data between the node and the next node in the loop

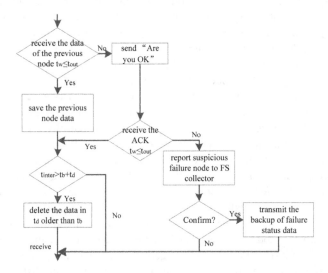

Fig. 7. The flow chart of receiving data and failure node judgment between the node and the previous node in the loop

DOWN, IDLE and so on. There is a problem that the node state which SLURM recorded is not timely or completely accurate.

The staffs who maintain the machine record the compute node state accurately but not timely. Based on the above, FS collector integrates the three methods to determine the node state as the Table 1 shows.

Table 1. Node state determination method of FS collector

RS collector	SLURM	Maintenance staffs	FS collector
Alarm	Normal	No	Normal, if SLURM state of the node turned to abnormal then change the node state to failure
Alarm	Abnormal	No	Failure
Normal	Abnormal	No	Normal, if the RS collector state of the node turned to abnormal then change the node state to failure
Any	Any	Abnormal	Failure
Remark	Abnormal states in SLURM includes DOWN(*) and ERROR(*), while others are normal states.		

4   Evaluation

This section focuses on the evaluations of DDC data collection framework. The Tianhe-1A supercomputer which the DDC runs on is detailed in Table 2.

Table 2. Specifications of Tianhe-1A

Item	Configuration
CPU	Xeon X5670 6C 2.93 GHz
Compute nodes amount	7168
Memory	229,376 GB
Interconnect	Proprietary(optic-electronic hybrid fat-tree structure, point to point bandwidth 160 Gbps)
Storage	Lustre(Lustre*4, total capacity 4 PB)
Operating system	Kylin Linux
SMC amount	448
Data collection interval	10 s

4.1   Hardware Status Data

Tables 3 and 4 show the data of ES collector collected from the sensors on the components of Tianhe-1A supercomputer including fans, communication board of frame (NRM), communication board of compute node (PDP), power supply, compute node mainboard and so on.

Table 3. Data collection from a single compute node

Attributes name	Type	Value	Unit
12 V	Voltage	11.98	V
Vbat	Voltage	3.28	V
ICH-1.5 V	Voltage	1.52	V
IOH-1.1 V	Voltage	1.13	V
5 V	Voltage	5.10	V
5Vsb	Voltage	5.08	V
3.3 V	Voltage	3.33	V
3.3Vsb	Voltage	3.30	V
CPU0 core	Voltage	0.90	V
CPU0 DR3-1.5 V	Voltage	1.54	V
CPU0 Temp	Temperature	29.00	C
CPU1 core	Voltage	0.95	V
CPU1 DDR3-1.5 V	Voltage	1.55	V
CPU1 Temp	Temperature	27.00	C
Thrm	Temperature	28.00	C
PDP-3.3 V	Voltage	3.3	V
PDP-2.5 V	Voltage	2.5	V
PDP-1.8 V	Voltage	1.8	V
PDP-1.5 V	Voltage	1.5	V
PDP-1.2 V	Voltage	1.2	V
PDP-Temperature	Temperature	40	C

4.2   Compute Node Running Status Data

The selected 136 data attributes collected by RS collector are divided into the following four parts: CPU related, Memory related, Network related and I/O related showed in Table 5.

4.3   ES Collector Overhead

ES collector collects and stores the hardware status data using dedicated Ethernet rather than Tianhe-1A high-speed interconnection network, so there is no overhead to the applications running on the compute nodes. Therefore, we tested the ES collector's performance overhead to the manager node by running the ps and vmstat command repeatedly and averaging the results. Table 6 shows the overhead of the manager node when ES collector collected data from 448 SMC servers (all of the Tianhe-1A SMCs). Figure 8 shows the overhead variation of ES collector with the different system scale for data collection. It is easy to find that the ES collector has little impact to the manager node and good scalability.

Table 4. Data collection from other components of the same frame

Component	Attributes name	Type	Value	Unit
Fan	Fan00 ~ Fan25	Fan	5763	RPM
Remark	In one frame 3 fan groups and 6 fans in each group			
NRM	12 V	Voltage	11.94	V
	3.3 V	Voltage	3.33	V
	STB3.3 V	Voltage	3.33	V
	Temp	Temperature	20.00	C
Remark	One NRM in each frame used for interconnection			
Power Supply	Temp	Temperature	48.00	C
	Fan1	Fan	1950	RPM
	Fan2	Fan	2100	RPM
	Input voltage	Voltage	222.00	V
	Input current	Current	2.59	A
	Output voltage	Voltage	11.97	V
	Output current	Current	40.00	A
Remark	Four power supplys in each frame			
SMC	1.8 V	Voltage	1.85	C
	STB3.3 V	Voltage	3.32	V
	5 V	Voltage	5.01	V
	12 V	Voltage	12.06	V
	Board Temp	Temperature	20.00	C
	Inlet Temp	Temperature	20.38	C
	Outlet1 Temp	Temperature	33.13	C
	Outlet2 Temp	Temperature	21.94	C
Remark	One SMC in each frame			

4.4   RS Collector Overhead

Table 7 presents the data collection overhead of RS collector on each node which is the average results by running ps command several times. When the data collection process collected or transmitted data, the average CPU utility rate was less than 0.6 %. The process did not take up CPU resources in the collection interval, so the average CPU utility rate was 0.06 % for each collection circulation. Data collection process of RS collector used 9.0 MB virtual memory, 1.1 MB physical memory and less than 1 ms to transmit the data to the next node. So the average bandwidth taken up by data transmission in 10 s is approximately 0.14 KB/s.

The data volume of each data collection for compute node running status data is about 700B. According to 10 s collection interval and the operation of deleting more than 3 h data every hour (t_b = 3 h, t_d = 1 h), the maximum amount of stored data is approximately 2 MB (1 MB for node itself, while 1 MB for backing up the previous node). All these overheads were at a low level.

Table 5. The compute node running status

Item	Attribute category	Amount
CPU related	CPU utilization	12
	Task creation and system switching activity	2
	Interrupt statistics	1
	Queue length and load averages	6
Memory related	Paging statistics	9
	Memory statistics	13
Network related	network statistics (devices, EDEV, SOCK, IP, EIP, ICMP, EICMP, TCP, ETCP, UDP)	78
I/O related	I/O and transfer rate statistics	5
	Status of inode	4
	Lustre statistics	6

Table 6. ES collector overhead of the manager node

CPU(%)	PhyMem(MB)	VirMem(MB)	I/O(MB/s)
0.4	5.8	67.5	3.8

Table 7. RS collector overhead of the compute node

CPU(%)	PhMem (MB)	VirMem (MB)	Data transmission time(s)	Bandwidth (KB/s)	Memory usage for data storage (MB)
Collecting < 0.6 Collection interval = 0	1.1	9.0	<0.001	0.14	2

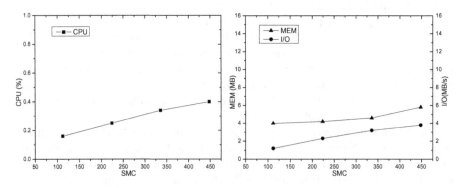

Fig. 8. Scalability test of ES collector

5 Conclusions and Future Work

This paper presents DDC data collection framework for failure prediction in Tianhe supercomputers. DDC adopts a distributed data collection architecture which can fully collect the data related to the compute nodes' health with little overhead. Through the testing for DDC which ran on TH-1A, the results indicated that DDC had the advantage of low cost and good scalability.

In the future, we will focus on the work related to data preprocessing and failure prediction model optimization. We will run the entire proactive fault-tolerance system firstly in Tianhe-1A.

Acknowledgments. This paper is supported by the National Natural Science Foundation of China (NSFC) No. 61272141, No. 61120106005 and the National High Technology Research and Development Program of China (863 Program) No. 2012AA01A301.

References

1. Yang, X., Wang, Z., Xue, J., Zhou, Y.: The reliability wall for exascale supercomputing. IEEE Trans. Comput. **61**(6), 767–779 (2012)
2. Philp, I.R.: Software failures and the road to a petaflop machine. In: Proceedings of the 1st Workshop on High Performance Computing Reliability Issues, San Francisco, CA, USA (2005)
3. Chen, Y., Plank, J.S., Li, K.: CLIP: a checkpointing tool for message-passing parallel programs. In: SC 1997, NY, USA (1997)
4. Hargrove, P.H., Duell, J.C.: Berkeley lab checkpoint/restart (BLCR) for Linux clusters. J. Phys: Conf. Ser. **46**(1), 494–499 (2006)
5. Liang, Y., Zhang, Y., Sivasubramaniam, A., Jette, M., Sahoo, R.: BlueGene/L failure analysis and prediction models. In: DSN 2006, Washington, DC, USA, pp. 425–434 (2006)
6. Liang, Y., Zhang, Y., Xiong, H., Sahoo, R.: Failure prediction in IBM BlueGene/L event logs. In: The Seventh IEEE International Conference on Data Mining, pp. 583–588 (2007)
7. Liang, Y., Zhang, Y., Xiong, H., Sahoo, R.: An adaptive semantic filter for Blue Gene/L failure log analysis. In: IEEE International Parallel and Distributed Processing Symposium, pp. 1–8 (2007)
8. Li, Y., Lan, Z.: Exploit failure prediction for adaptive fault-tolerance in cluster computing. In: CCGRID 2006, Washington, DC, USA, pp. 531–538 (2006)
9. Lan, Z., Gu, J., Zheng, Z., Thakur, R., Coghlan, S.: A study of dynamic meta-learning for failure prediction in large-scale systems. J. Parallel Distrib. Comput. **70**(6), 630–643 (2010)
10. Zheng, Z., Yu, L., Tang, W., Lan, Z., Gupta, R., Desai, N., Coghlan, S., Buettner, D.: Co-analysis of RAS log and job log on Blue Gene/P. In: IPDPS 2011, pp. 840–851 (2011)
11. Sahoo, R.K., Oliner, A.J., Rish, I., Gupta, M., Moreira, J.E., Ma, S., Vilalta, R., Sivasubramaniam, A.: Critical event prediction for proactive management in large-scale computer clusters. In: KDD 2003, NY, USA, pp. 426–435 (2003)
12. Oliner, A., Rudolph, L., Sahoo, R.: Cooperative checkpointing theory. In: IPDPS 2006, Washington, DC, USA, pp. 132–141 (2006)
13. Oliner, A., Ganapathi, A., Xu, W.: Advances and challenges in log analysis. Commun. ACM **55**(2), 55–61 (2012)

14. Yamanishi, K., Maruyama, Y.: Dynamic syslog mining for network failure monitoring. In: KDD 2005, New York, NY, USA, pp. 499–508 (2005)
15. Xu, W., Huang, L., Fox, A., Patterson, D., Jordan, M.I.: Detecting large-scale system problems by mining console logs. In: SOSP 2009, NY, USA, pp. 117–132 (2009)
16. Vaarandi, R.: A breadth-first algorithm for mining frequent patterns from event logs. In: Aagesen, F.A., Anutariya, C., Wuwongse, V. (eds.) INTELLCOMM 2004. LNCS, vol. 3283, pp. 293–308. Springer, Heidelberg (2004)
17. Gainaru, A., Cappello, F., Snir, M., Kramer, W.: Fault prediction under the microscope: a closer look into HPC systems. In: SC 2012, Los Alamitos, CA, USA (2012)
18. Scott, S.L., Engelmann, C., Vallee, G.R., Naughton, T., Tikotekar, A., Ostrouchov, G., et al.: A tunable holistic resiliency approach for high-performance computing systems. In: PPoPP 2009, NY, USA, pp. 305–306 (2009)
19. Nagarajan, A.B., Mueller, F., Engelmann, C., Scott, S.L.: Proactive fault tolerance for HPC with Xen virtualization. In: ICS 2007, NY, USA, pp. 23–32 (2007)
20. Rajachandrasekar, R., Besseron, X., Panda, D.K.: Monitoring and predicting hardware failures in HPC clusters with FTB-IPMI. In: IEEE 26th International Parallel and Distributed Processing Symposium Workshops PhD Forum (IPDPSW), pp. 1136–1143 (2012)
21. Buyya, R.: PARMON: a portable and scalable monitoring system for clusters. Softw. Pract. Exper. 30(7), 723–739 (2000)
22. Massie, M.L., Chun, B.N., Culler, D.E.: The ganglia distributed monitoring system: design, implementation, and experience. Parallel Comput. 30(7), 817–840 (2004)
23. Brandt, J.M., Debusschere, B.J., Gentile, A.C., Mayo, J.R., Pebay, P.P., Thompson, D., et al.: Ovis-2: a robust distributed architecture for scalable RAS. In: IEEE International Symposium on Parallel and Distributed Processing, pp. 1–8 (2008)

Optimizing the MapReduce Framework for CPU-MIC Heterogeneous Cluster

Wenzhu Wang$^{(\boxtimes)}$, Qingbo Wu, Yusong Tan, and Yaoxue Zhang

College of Computer, National University of Defense Technology, Changsha, China
{wenzhuw,wu.qingbo2008,yusong.tan}@gmail.com, zyx@csu.edu.cn

Abstract. MapReduce is a distributed programming paradigm to process large scale data set. Meanwhile, with the development of coprocessors, heterogeneous architecture is widely used for getting high performance. Therefore, it is natural to try to leverage both of them for big data processing. In this paper, we propose an optimized MapReduce framework for CPU-MIC heterogeneous Cluster, which mainly provides the following new features: First, a runtime is developed for MIC management, fault tolerance, and task scheduling. Second, we design SIMD friendly map and pipelined reduce to improve the efficiency of resources utilization. In addition, a memory management scheme is implemented for accessing <key, value> pairs on MIC efficiently. The experimental results show that our system is up to 2.4x and 8.1x faster than Hadoop for different applications.

Keywords: MapReduce · Hadoop · Many Integrated Core · Big Data

1 Introduction

With the explosion of digital data, Big Data has become a hot topic in many domains. However, one challenge is that how to dig the huge value from the large scale data set whin an acceptable time. To deal with this urge, MapReduce framework [1] is proposed by Google, which could process a huge data set by utilizing the computing resources in parallel. Moreover, developers only need to write the map and reduce functions, and the other works are handled by MapReduce runtime automatically. Therefore, the open-source implementations, such as Hadoop and Spark, have been widely used in internet enterprises and research communities.

The original goal of MapReduce is to employ the power of common CPU clusters. However, with the high speed development of coprocessors, such as GPU, FPGA, and coupled CPU-GPU, several studies have implemented MapReduce framework on these platforms [3,9,10]. Especially, Many Integrated Core (MIC) is a new kind of coprocessor designed by Intel Corporation, which has great computing power and friendly programming models [5,6]. Compared with CPU and GPU, MIC also has several new characteristics, such as wider Vector Process Units (VPU), more on-chip threads, and higher memory bandwidth. As a result, the MapReduce framework for MIC architecture has also been studied [7,8].

© Springer International Publishing Switzerland 2015
Y. Chen et al. (Eds.): APPT 2015, LNCS 9231, pp. 33–44, 2015.
DOI: 10.1007/978-3-319-23216-4_3

In this paper, we focus on utilizing the power of CPU-MIC heterogeneous cluster in MapReduce framework to process large scale data set more efficiently. Different from the former works on MIC, our framework is a library with several new features, and can be integrated into Hadoop or other MapReduce systems. However, we also met some challenges during the system exploitation, such as heterogeneous cluster management, utilizing the VPUs on MIC, and MIC memory management, etc. Thus, we try to address these challenges in the system design, and mainly make the following contributions.

- We design a **MIC token** mechanism for the scalability and fault tolerance of MIC management. It could manage the MIC coprocessors in flexible ways, such as handling the MIC failure, and dealing with the dynamical change of MIC in the cluster.
- For using MIC easily, we provide several user APIs, such as buffer allocation, task transfer, and hash combine. Moreover, we develop SIMD friendly map for utilizing the VPUs on MIC in the map phase efficiently.
- To reduce the data storage size in MIC memory, we design a Hash Combine stage on MIC, which could combine the <key, value> pairs with the same key between all threads. The hash combine operation uses low cost synchronous operations and efficient SIMD hash algorithm to make the key indexing $O(1)$ time complexity.
- Pipelined reduce is designed to improve the efficiency of resource utilization, in which MICs run the map tasks, and CPUs run the reduce tasks in a pipeline manner. It could overlap parts of the map and reduce time and improve the system throughput.
- Finally, an efficient memory management scheme is designed for MIC memory allocation, in which several types of buffer can be used by users. The Array Buffer has no synchronization overhead but a large memory space, while the Combine Buffer has a low synchronization overhead but a small memory space. Meanwhile, the task buffer is designed for storing the map tasks. All buffers are scalable for multi-threads and reused during a job running.

A prototype system is implemented on a CPU-MIC heterogeneous cluster, which includes 8 CPUs and 6 MIC coprocessors. To compare the performance of our system, a CPU cluster with 8 CPUs is also built up. We run four common MapReduce benchmarks on CPU-MIC and CPU cluster respectively. The experimental results show that our system is up to 2.4x and 8.1x faster than Hadoop for different applications.

The rest of this paper is organized as follows: The MIC architecture and MapReduce framework are introduced in Sect. 2. Section 3 gives the details of system design and implementation. Section 4 evaluates the performance of our system compared with Hadoop for different applications. Finally, we conclude this paper in Sect. 5.

2   Background

2.1   Intel MIC Architecture

Many Integrated Core (MIC) architecture has 50+ x86 cores, and each core supports four hardware threads running on a dual in-order execution pipeline. The multiple threads running in round-robin manner could hide the latencies of in-order instruction execution. There are 512-bit width Vector Processing Units (VPUs) for SIMD (Single Instruction Multi Data) processing on each core. In addition, each core has 32K L1 data cache, 32K L1 instruction cache, and 512 KB L2 cache. The high speed bi-directional ring connecting all L2 caches could improve the cache efficiency by trying to access data from other core's L2 cache directly. Because of no L3 cache, the penalty of cache miss is as high as about 200 cycles. However, it has high memory bandwidth and memory speed, which are about 350 GB/s and 5GT/s.

MIC mainly supports two programming models: native and offload. In native model, MIC can be seen as an independent SMP computing system. The software stack provides many interface supports standard APIs, such as TCP/IP and MPI communication interface. In offload model, MIC works as a coprocessor and connects with CPU via PCIe bus. The data and program transferred to MIC are initiated and controlled by host CPU. Because CPU and MIC share different memory address space, programmers need to manage two copies of data on both sides. Both of the programming models need to utilize the multithread program models, such as OpenMP, TBB, Cilk, and OpenCL.

2.2   MapReduce

MapReduce is a distributed programming framework for processing large scale data set in ordinary CPU clusters. In this programming model, developers mainly need to write two serial functions: map and reduce. Other works, such as data distribution, parallel processing, fault tolerance, and load balance, are handled by MapReduce runtime in transparent manners.

The map and reduce functions are both defined with restricted data structure of <key, value> pairs. Firstly, the Map function maps a pair of input data to another data domain:

$$\textbf{\textit{Map:}} < k1, v1 > \rightarrow < k2, v2 >$$

After map stage, the runtime shuffles all the intermediate results and groups the <key, value> pairs according to the value of key. Then, the Reduce function is executed for each group and produces a collection of values in the same key:

$$\textbf{\textit{Reduce:}} < k2, \text{list}(v2) > \rightarrow \text{list}(v3)$$

With the rapid development of coprocessors, many studies for adapting MapReduce framework on CPU-coprocessor architecture have emerged. Researches [3,9–11] optimize the MapReduce framework on single GPU coprocessor, and [4, 12–14] leverage GPU clusters to run MapReduce for large scale data processing. There are also similar studies on other processors, like multi-core system [15, 16], IBM Cell [17], and Intel MIC [7].

MRPhi [7] is the first work to optimize the MapReduce framework on MIC. The extension work [8] could run on a heterogeneous platform equipped with multiple MIC processors, and MPI is used to coordinate the communication between the host and MIC. Different from MRPhi, in our framework, MIC is only used to speed up the map tasks, and reduce tasks are run on CPU in pipeline manner. Moreover, our framework could be integrated into other MapReduce systems, like Hadoop and Spark, and utilize the HDFS and Yarn to get more benefits.

3   Design and Implementation

This section introduces the design and implementation of our system, including the overall framework, SIMD friendly map, pipelined reduce, and memory management scheme, etc. Overall, the goal of our work is to utilize the power of CPU-MIC cluster to process large scale data set in efficient, fault tolerant, and easy programming ways.

3.1   The Overall Framework

Like other MapReduce frameworks, the overall workflow of our system includes task distribution, map, shuffle, and reduce, etc. The most difference is that the tasks are not only processed by CPUs, but also by MIC coprocessors. Figure 1 shows the overall framework. The job manager manages a MapReduce job. When a new job comes, it splits the job into small tasks firstly. As MIC has an outstanding computing power, each task is large enough to fill up the computing units of MIC and get desirable speedups. Therefore, one task usually contains one or more input files.

There are two types of worker in each node: CPU worker and MIC worker. The CPU worker is the normal MapReduce worker for running the map and reduce tasks. In contrast, the MIC worker is a MIC manager. It transfers a new map task to MIC, and receives the results produced by MIC. As the CPU and MIC have different computing power, we allocate the tasks dynamically. When a CPU/MIC worker is idle, the job manager allocates a new task to it. Dynamic task allocation could avoid loading imbalance between all workers.

For system scalability and fault tolerance, we design a **MIC token** mechanism. The runtime probes the usability of each MIC in a heartbeat-based communication mechanism, and allocates each available MIC a unique token. A MIC worker must get a token before transferring a new task to MIC. Furthermore, the token could be changed dynamically with the MIC coprocessors changing in cluster. Meanwhile, some MICs may be failed because of PCIe bus failed or offload service stopped. When a MIC is failed, the according token is also deleted.

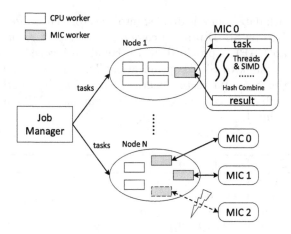

Fig. 1. The overall framework

For example, in Fig. 1, Node N has three MIC tokens at first. However, when MIC 2 is failed, the runtime will detect the failure and delete the according token.

The CPU worker and MIC worker could transform into each other. If a CPU worker gets a token, it will become a MIC worker. In contrast, if a MIC worker loses the token, it will also transform into a CPU worker. In Fig. 1, the MIC worker, managing the MIC 2 in Node N, will transform into a normal CPU worker when losing the MIC token.

To use the power of MIC easily, we provide several user APIs for MIC usage, including buffer allocation, task transfer, and hash combine. Furthermore, we relax the constraint of map function, so users can optimize the MIC codes further according to the specific application, such as thread affinity, high-level MIC instructions, etc. As there are hundreds of threads on MIC to process one map task simultaneously, the task needs to be split into many small data chunks, so all thread could process the data chunks in parallel.

In our system, MIC processors only process the map tasks, and reduce tasks only processed by CPU workers. Note that CPUs can also process the map tasks simultaneously. The main reason is that the reduce phase mainly includes the memory-intensive, branch, and data retrieval operations, which are not efficient running on MIC. Moreover, running reduce on MIC incurs another data transfer overhead between CPU and MIC. By this way, pipelined map and reduce could utilize different system resources efficiently. Finally, CPU workers run the reduce phase and output the final results.

3.2 SIMD Friendly Map

The performance obtained from MIC depends on the utilization of VPUs greatly. Therefore, we design SIMD friendly map for running map tasks on MIC. As described above, each thread on MIC process several data chunks of a map task.

In our system, each data chunk is divided into a vector. Therefore, a data chunk could use the VPUs by SIMD pragma command, such as # *pragma ivdep*.

The MIC_map() API is provided, which could be invoked by developer to process each data chunk by SIMD optimization. The parameters include a data chunk d_i, a integer α, and a vector length l, where l is the length of VPUs in MIC, and the length of data chunk d_i is $\alpha * l$. An example of MIC_map() function is given in Algorithm 1.

Algorithm 1. SIMD friendly map

1: MIC_map(d_i, α, l) {
2: **for** m=0; m< $\alpha * l$; m+=l **do**
3:    #pragma ivdep
4:    SIMD_Process($d_i[m : m + l - 1]$)
5:    MIC_vector_emit(Key_vector, Value_vector, l)
6: **end for**
7: }

In Algorithm 1, data chunk d_i is processed α times, and each time is optimized by SIMD operation. After processing d_i, the results contain a key vector and a value vector. The MIC_vector_emit() function is provided for storing them as <key, value> pairs in MIC memory. During the map phase on MIC, all data chunks are processed by hundreds of threads on MIC in parallel.

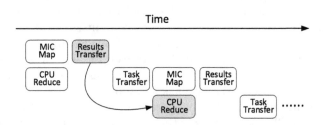

Fig. 2. Pipelined reduce

3.3 Pipelined Reduce

The reduce function mainly includes memory-intensive, branch and data retrieval operations, which are not efficient running on MIC. Therefore, we execute the reduce phase on CPU rather than MIC. Meanwhile, running reduce on CPU can also avoid the data transfer overhead of reduce tasks between CPU and MIC.

The reduce workers on CPUs are running in pipeline manner. When a map task is finished by MIC, the intermediate results are copied back into host memory through PCIe bus. Then, MIC worker could continue to process another map

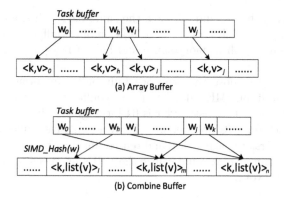

Fig. 3. MIC memory management

task without waiting. At the same time, the reduce workers shuffle and reduce the intermediate results. By this way, the map and reduce workers could be running simultaneously, and improve the overall throughput by using different resources.

The pipelined reduce can be illustrated as Fig. 2. We can see that the map and reduce phases are overlapped. Meanwhile, the reduce workers process the results copied in the previous cycle, as the grey parts shown, so the reduce wokers don't need to wait the results transfer. Note that when MIC workers are running, the CPU workers can also execute the map tasks. In the reduce phase, the runtime distributes all reduce tasks among reduce workers evenly for avoiding data skew, and collects all reduce results as the final output results.

3.4   Memory Management Scheme

In the map phase, all threads running on MIC store their intermediate <key, value> pairs in MIC memory simultaneously. Therefore, the synchronization overhead is a potential bottleneck during this process. To handle this challenge, we design two types of result buffer for storing results efficiently: Array Buffer and Combine Buffer.

In the Array Buffer, shown as Fig. 3(a), each element w_i in the task has a unique position, <key, value>$_i$, to store its result. Although Array Buffer occupies a large space, it has no locks or atomic operations for threads synchronization. Array Buffer is applicable when there is no combining operations, or combining operation can't save much memory space.

In the Combine Buffer, shown as Fig. 3(b), all threads on MIC share the same memory space for results storing. When using this buffer, multiple threads may access the same position at the same time. Therefore, we use a low cost synchronous operation, which is well supported on MIC architecture without significant overhead. Furthermore, the probability of accessing the same position at the same time is very low in most applications, as the range of hash value is very large. In Fig. 3(b), w_i and w_k have the same hash value, and their values are combined into the $<k,\text{list}(v)>_n$. In brief, Combine Buffer is applicable when combining can save much memory space and have a low probability of conflict on hash value.

Developers could choose the type of result buffer in terms of the specific application. In addition, MIC also has a task buffer to store the tasks transferred from host node. The task buffer is 64-bit aligned, which could get a high performance based on MIC architecture. To avoid massive requests for memory allocation, all buffers are page-locked and reused during job running. Moreover, a SIMD hash algorithm, which could utilize the VPUs for speeding up, is provided for developers to invoke.

4   Experimental Evaluation

In this section, we evaluate the performance of our system in a CPU-MIC cluster with Hadoop in an ordinary CPU cluster. Our system is integrated into Hadoop, so we can utilize the HDFS and Yarn. Firstly, we introduce the experimental setup, including hardware platform configuration and testing programs. Then, we show the comparing results for different applications.

4.1   Experimental Setup

We deploy a CPU-MIC cluster and an ordinary CPU cluster respectively. The CPU-MIC cluster includes 4 computing nodes, which equiped with 8 CPUs and 6 MICs. The MIC coprocessor is Intel Xeon Phi 3120P, which has 6 GB memory, 57 cores working at 1.1 GHz, and 512-bit VPUs on each core. In contrast, the CPU cluster includes 4 computing nodes with 8 CPUs. The CPU is Intel Xeon E5-2670, which has 8 cores working at 2.6 GHz.

Others configuration: The host memory is 136G, and the hard drive is a 500G SATA3 magnetic hard disk. The 64 bit RedHat 6.2 is used as the operating system, and Intel composer_xe_2013 is used as the compile environment.

We use four common MapReduce benchmarks to evaluate the system performance: K-Means, Matrix Multiplication, Principal Component Analysis, and Word Count. To reflect the impact of different data size, we use three kinds of data set: Small (S), Medium (M) and Large (L). Table. 1 shows the description of these different size we used for each application.

Table 1. The data size used for applications.

Application	Data sets		
K-Means	S:480M	M:4.8G	L:48G
Matrix Multiplication	S:480M	M:4.8G	L:48G
Principal Component Analysis	S:480M	M:4.8G	L:48G
Word Count	S:1.36G	M:13.6G	L:136G

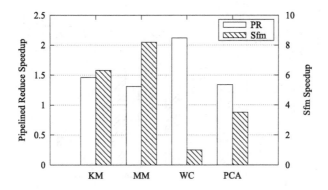

Fig. 4. Speedup of optimization techniques

4.2   Benchmark Implementation

We implement these four benchmarks in Hadoop firstly, and then implement them in our system. The implementation are described briefly as follows.

K-Means (KM): K-Means clustering is a method of grouping thousands of items into k groups. Each map task contains n items. The map task calculates the distance from each item to all central nodes of the k groups, then finds the group with the minimum distance to the given item. The reduce task sums all items within the same group and recalculates the central node. The map and reduce stage won't stop until all the central nodes aren't changed anymore or reach the iteration number predefined.

Matrix Multiplication (MM): Matrix Multiplication is a binary operation that a pair of matrices produces another matrix, which has been widely used in eigenvalue analysis. In a map task, m rows from the first matrix and n columns from the second matrix are multiplied, then all the outputs are summed up as the final result. The reduce stage isn't required in this application.

Principal Component Analysis (PCA): Principal Component Analysis is a statistical procedure that uses orthogonal transformation to convert a set of observations of possibly correlated variables into a set of values of linearly uncorrelated variables called principal components. The Map function computes the covariance of an element, and then emits the covariance as the value according to the element index. The Reduce function computes the identity of the results.

Word Count (WC): Word Count counts the number of each word in a collection of document files. A map task contains a set of data read from the input files, and gives each key a value of 1. The same keys in the intermediate results could be combined after map stage. The reduce task counts the number of each word collected from the map stage.

4.3   Experimental Results

Firstly, we evaluate the performance impact of the optimization techniques, including the SIMD friendly map and pipelined reduce. Figure 4 shows the

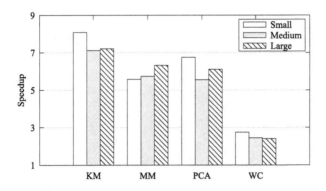

Fig. 5. Speedup over CPU cluster

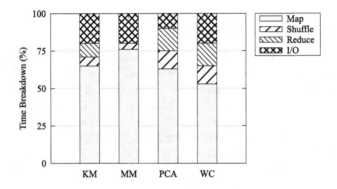

Fig. 6. Time breakdown

evaluation results. For pipelined reduce (PR), the speedup is up to 1.18x and 1.39x. The Word Count can get more benefits from it, as there is more proportion of I/O and reduce phases during the execution. For SIMD friendly map (Sfm), the speedup is up to 1.0x and 8.2. K-Means can get the best performance, as Hadoop can hardly utilize the VPUs in map phase, while Sfm can use them efficiently. Especially, Word Count gets little benefit from Sfm, as there is no SIMD operations in the map phase.

Then, we compare our system running on the CPU-MIC cluster with Hadoop running on the ordinary CPU cluster. The experimental results are illustrated in Fig. 5. Overall, our system could achieve up to 2.4x and 8.1x speedups over Hadoop for different applications and data sizes. For K-Means, Matrix Multiplication, and Principal Component Analysis, they can get higher speedups than Word Count, as these application have more SIMD operations in map phase to utilize the VPUs on MIC. In contrast, Word Count takes little advantage of VPUs. However, it is still able to utilize the multiple threads on MIC and get a desirable speedup.

Finally, we illustrate the time breakdown of these benchmarks in Fig. 6. For K-Means and Matrix Multiplication, the main time is in the map phase, as these two applications have much computing in map. In contrast, for Word Count, the shuffle, reduce, and I/O occupy a large time proportion, which is mainly because string processing produces lots of <key, value> pairs and need to be processed by these operations.

5   Conclusion and Future Work

With the rapid development of high performance coprocessors and Big Data, many studies have tried to utilize the advantages of both of them in Big Data processing. As MIC is a new kind of coprocessor with remarkable computing power, we design and implement an efficient, fault tolerant, and easy programming MapReduce framework for CPU-MIC heterogeneous cluster. Our system has a runtime to manage the MIC coprocessors in fault tolerance and flexible ways, an efficient SIMD friendly map and pipelined reduce design, and a memory management scheme for accessing <key, value> pairs on MIC. The experimental results have shown that our system has an exciting performance on CPU-MIC cluster compared with Hadoop.

The future work includes improving the system programmability, optimizing MIC memory management, improving the utilization of system resources further, and scaling our system on larger CPU-MIC clusters.

References

1. Dean, J., Ghemawat, S.: MapReduce: simplified data processing on large clusters. Commun. ACM **51**(1), 107–113 (2008)
2. Appuswamy, R., Gkantsidis, C., Narayanan, D., Hodson, O., Rowstron, A.: Scale-up vs scale-out for hadoop: time to rethink? In: Proceedings of the 4th annual Symposium on Cloud Computing, p. 20. ACM Press (2013)
3. He, B., Fang, W., Luo, Q., Govindaraju, N.K., Wang, T.: Mars: a MapReduce framework on graphics processors. In: Proceedings of the 17th international conference on Parallel architectures and compilation techniques, pp. 260–269. ACM Press, Toronto (2008)
4. Stuart, J.A., Owens, J.D.: Multi-GPU MapReduce on GPU clusters. In: 25th IEEE International Parallel & Distributed Processing Symposium, pp. 1068–1079. IEEE Press, Anchorage, Alaska (2011)
5. Heinecke, A., Klemm, M., Pflger, D., Bode, A., Bungartz, H.J.: Extending a highly parallel data mining algorithm to the Intel® many integrated core architecture. In: Alexander, M., et al. (eds.) Euro-Par 2011. LNCS, vol. 7156, pp. 375–384. Springer, Heidelberg (2012)
6. Schulz, K.W., Ulerich, R., Malaya, N., Bauman, P.T., Stogner, R., Simmons, C.: Early experiences porting scientific applications to the Many Integrated Core (MIC) platform. In: TACC-Intel Highly Parallel Computing Symposium, Austin, Texas (2012)

7. Lu, M., Zhang, L., Huynh, H.P., Ong, Z., Liang, Y., He, B., Huynh, R.: Optimizing the MapReduce framework on Intel Xeon Phi coprocessor. In: International Conference on Big Data, pp. 125–130. IEEE Press, Santa Clara, California (2013)

8. Lu, M., Liang, Y., Huynh, H., Liang, O., He, B., Goh, R.: MrPhi: an optimized MapReduce framework on Intel Xeon Phi Coprocessors. IEEE Trans. Parallel Distrib. Syst. **PP**(99), 1 (2014)

9. Basaran, C., Kang, K.D.: Grex: an efficient MapReduce framework for graphics processing units. J. Parallel Distrib. Comput. **73**(4), 522–533 (2013)

10. Hong, C., Chen, D., Chen, W., Zheng, W., Lin, H.: MapCG: writing parallel program portable between CPU and GPU. In: Proceedings of the 19th International Conference on Parallel Architectures and Compilation Techniques, pp. 217–226. ACM Press, Vienna (2010)

11. Chen, L., Huo, X., Agrawal, G.: Accelerating MapReduce on a coupled CPU-GPU architecture. In: International Conference for High Performance Computing, Networking, Storage and Analysis, p. 25. IEEE Press, Salt Lake, Utah (2012)

12. Farivar, R., Verma, A., Chan, E.M., Campbell, R.H.: Mithra: multiple data independent tasks on a heterogeneous resource architecture. In: IEEE International Conference on Cluster Computing, pp. 1–10. IEEE Press, New Orleans, Louisiana (2009)

13. Chen, Y., Qiao, Z., Jiang, H., Li, K.-C., Ro, W.W.: MGMR: Multi-GPU based MapReduce. In: Park, J.J.J.H., Arabnia, H.R., Kim, C., Shi, W., Gil, J.-M. (eds.) GPC 2013. LNCS, vol. 7861, pp. 433–442. Springer, Heidelberg (2013)

14. Fang, W., He, B., Luo, Q., Govindaraju, N.K.: Mars: accelerating MapReduce with graphics processors. IEEE Trans. Parallel Distrib. Syst. **22**(4), 608–620 (2011)

15. Ranger, C., Raghuraman, R., Penmetsa, A., Bradski, G., Kozyrakis, C.: Evaluating MapReduce for multi-core and multiprocessor systems. In: IEEE 13th International Symposium on High Performance Computer Architecture, pp. 13–24. IEEE Press, Phoenix, Arizona (2007)

16. Talbot, J., Yoo, R. M., Kozyrakis, C.: Phoenix++: modular MapReduce for shared-memory systems. In: Proceedings of the second international workshop on MapReduce and its applications, pp. 9–16. ACM Press, San Jose, California (2011)

17. de Kruijf, M., Sankaralingam, K..: MapReduce for the Cell BE architecture. University of Wisconsin Computer Sciences Technical Report CS-TR-2007-1625 (2007)

Stable Matching Scheduler for Single-ISA Heterogeneous Multi-core Processors

Lei Wang[1,2(⊠)], Shaoli Liu[1], Chao Lu[1,2], Longbing Zhang[1,3],
Junhua Xiao[3], and Jian Wang[1,3]

[1] Key Laboratory of Computer Architecture,
Institute of Computing Technology, Chinese Academy of Sciences,
Beijing, China
wanglei-cpu@ict.ac.cn
[2] University of Chinese Academy of Sciences, Beijing, China
[3] Loongson Technology Corporation Limited, Beijing, China

Abstract. The overall performance of single-ISA heterogeneous multi-core processors (HMPs) heavily relies on the efficiency of scheduling algorithm. However, traditional scheduling algorithms either treat all cores equally, or assume all cores complying with a strict order in the amount of microarchitecture resources, thus it is unsuitable for increasingly diverse HMPs, where different cores may have different advantages and preferences.

To efficiently schedule single-ISA HMPs, we propose a novel stable matching scheduler based on the matching game theory. The proposed scheduler can always lead to a stable matching between applications and cores, where there does not exist an alternative application-core pair in which both the application and the core prefer each other rather than their current partners. Experimental results demonstrate that the stable matching scheduler beats previous schedules. For example, the stable matching scheduler improves, on average, the performance against the random scheduler by 19.86 % (4-core), 18.78 % (6-core), 22.78 % (8-core).

Keywords: Single-ISA hmps · Scheduling · Multi-programmed workloads · Stable matching

1 Introduction

Homogeneous multi-core processors have become mainstream over the past few decades. However, applications with different characteristics are very likely to exhibit different architecture demands [1]. Heterogeneous multi-core processors (HMPs) were proposed [2–5] to satisfy those diverse architecture demands with less energy consumption. There are two different kinds of HMPs: single-ISA HMPs and non-identical-ISA HMPs.

Supported by the National Sci&Tech Major Project (No.2009ZX01028-002-003, 2009ZX01029-001-003, 2010ZX01036-001-002, 2012ZX01029-001-002-002, 2014ZX01020201, 2014ZX01030101), National Natural Science Foundation of China (No.61221062, 61133004, 61173001, 61232009, 61222204, 61432016), the National High Technology Development 863 Program of China (2012AA010901, 2013AA014301)

© Springer International Publishing Switzerland 2015
Y. Chen et al. (Eds.): APPT 2015, LNCS 9231, pp. 45–59, 2015.
DOI: 10.1007/978-3-319-23216-4_4

In single-ISA HMPs, all cores share the same ISA but differ in architecture features (e.g. issue width, cache size, frequency, etc.) [2, 3]. In non-identical-ISA HMPs, cores have non-identical ISAs [4, 5] and different architectures correspondingly. In this paper, we focus on single-ISA HMPs, since it maximizes the flexibility of scheduling.

The overall performance of single-ISA HMPs mainly relies on the efficiency of scheduling, which dynamically assigns applications to the appropriate cores. However, since the current operate system is unaware of the heterogeneity of architectures, the inefficient random algorithm and round-robin algorithm are the most frequently used [6].

To address this issue, Kumar et al. [7] proposed a heuristic sampling-based algorithm, which examines all the possible assignments in sampling phase and chooses the best assignment. Since the number of possible assignments grows factorially with the problem scale, the heuristic sampling-based algorithm is inefficient for large-scale system. Instead of exhaustively searching all possible assignments, greedy algorithm [8, 9, 12–14] makes the local optimized assignment for one core at a time by assigning application with better performance to core with more architecture resources. In general, the greedy scheduling algorithm is specially designed for systems where the cores maintain a monotonic relationship, both in design and performance - for example, the bigger core has more architecture resources in every dimension and provides better performance for every application than the smaller one. However, considering the increasingly diversity of heterogeneity in HMPs (e.g. the trend of application-specific cores), the assumption of a monotonic order of cores for different applications may not always hold [10]. In order to adapt to the development of HMPs architectures, it requires to design a more efficient scheduling algorithm.

We propose a novel scheduler which firstly identifies the design of scheduling problem with the matching game theory, which was developed by Gale and Shapley in the 1960s [15]. It is a theory about how to find a stable matching between two sets of individuals with the given preferences. Specifically, a matching is called stable when there does not exist any alternative pairing (A, B) in which both A and B prefer each other rather than the individuals to which they are currently matched. The marriage model and the college admission model were specially designed to explain the stable matching problem. Taking the marriage model as an example, the matching begins with each man proposing to his favorite woman. Then every woman compares all of the received proposals (if any), picks out the favorite one and rejects the others. The men who were rejected in the last round then propose to their next choices. Again, the women compare all of the received proposals (including the proposal picked out in the last round) and pick out the favorite. This continues until every man has been accepted by a woman. The process of reaching the stable assignment typically requires no more than $n^2 - 2n + 2$ iterations. Due to the success in both theory and practice, this work has been awarded the 2012 nobel prize for economic [16].

In the stable matching scheduler, to regard applications and cores as the two sets of individuals involved in the matching game, we need to know the preferences of each application and core, which are inferred by an Artificial Neural Networks (ANN) prediction model with limited hardware overhead. The detail of ANN prediction model will be described in Sect. 3.2.

We leverage three different HMPs (4-core, 6-core, 8-core) and select a number of representative benchmarks from the SPEC CPU2006 benchmark suite [17] to evaluate our scheduler. The proposed stable matching scheduler is compared against the random scheduler [6], the round robin scheduler [6, 11], the sampling-based scheduler [7] and the greedy scheduler [12, 14]. We observe from experiments that our scheduler achieves the best performance and energy efficiency (performance/power) across all scenarios considered. For example, compared with the random scheduler, the proposed stable matching scheduler averagely improves the performance by 19.86 % (4-core), 18.78 % (6-core), 22.78 % (8-core). Even compared with state-of-the-art greedy scheduler [12, 14], the stable matching scheduler reports performance improvement by 3.8 % (4-core), 4.9 % (6-core) and 9.7 % (8-core), respectively.

Our contributions are as follows. First, we firstly propose to apply the matching game theory to explore the scheduling problem in single-ISA HMPs, and propose a stable matching scheduler. Second, to predict the performance of applications on different cores, we choose to follow a state-of-the-art work [18] to construct a low cost hardware Artificial Neural Networks (ANN) prediction model. Third, the proposed scheduler achieves significant improvement on both performance and energy efficiency.

The rest of the paper is organized as follows: Sect. 2 reviews some related works about scheduling. Section 3 presents our scheduler in detail. Section 4 presents the experimental methodology and empirically evaluates our scheduler. Section 5 concludes this paper and discuss the future work.

2   Related Work

Previous researches studied the heterogeneous-aware scheduling from two aspects: the performance prediction model and the scheduling algorithm. In this section we briefly review these two categories of researches.

Performance Prediction. Kumar et al. proposed a heuristic sampling-based scheduler and demonstrated that heterogeneous architecture could deliver better performance and energy efficiency [7]. IPC-driven is a similar sampling-based approach which avoids to sample all possible assignments [9]. Winter et al. proposed a combinatorial optimization scheduler to coordinate applications scheduling and power management [14]. In general, the sampling-based schedulers introduce significant overhead due to the frequent migration of applications between cores. Moreover, such sampling overhead increases rapidly with the number of core types in the system.

To avoid the sampling overhead, a number of non-sample works were proposed. In [8, 13], the authors leveraged memory intensity such as cache miss rate or memory stalls to classify applications as memory-intensive or compute-intensive. Schedulers assign compute-intensive applications to the big cores for better performance and assign memory-intensive applications to the small cores for energy efficiency. Shelepov et al. proposed Heterogeneity-Aware Signature-Supported (HASS) which leverages architecture signatures embedded in the application binary to predict application performance [19]. In paper [20], the authors evaluate the influence of memory behavior on application performance by considering both the LLC miss rate and memory access patterns. Craeynest et al. showed that considering only memory behavior usually causes suboptimal scheduling [21].

Most previous studies took application behaviors (e.g.,cache miss rate) as the basis of prediction [8, 13, 19–21]. However, application behaviors are determined by soft ware, hardware, and their interaction. Considering all those factors in a mixed way requires very complex models. Wu et al. proposed to distinguish the influence of softwar and hardware on performance by considering only the architecture independent application characteristics [18]. This work simplifies the model specification. In this paper, we construct an ANN model to predict the performance of each application on each core type with the architecture independent application characteristics.

Scheduling Algorithm. Another important issue in scheduling is the scheduling algorithm. The random scheduler and the round-robin scheduler are frequently-used in current operating systems [6]. The random scheduler randomly assigns applications to cores. The round-robin scheduler ensures different core types are equally shared among the applications. In [11], the authors proposed to use the round-robin scheduler and Throughput-Driven Fairness (TDF) scheduler to improve the fairness in HMPs.

Exhaustive searching algorithm [7] simply tries all possible assignments and selects the best performed one. The most important limitation of exhaustive searching algorithm is its bad scalability. The number of candidate assignments grows factorially with the problem size. Therefore, exhaustive search is practical only for very small systems.

Greedy algorithm is another popular algorithm due to its simple implementation. In work [12, 14], the authors employed a scheduling algorithm called VarF&AppIPC that ranks the applications by relative IPC (instructions per cycle) and ranks the cores by architecture resources (frequencies), applications are assigned to cores according to their corresponding positions in rankings. Greedy strategy was also used in many other schedulers [8, 13, 19–21]. Greedy algorithms are most effective when there is a monotonic order of cores for all applications. However, since Kumar et al. [10] shows that such assumption may not always hold, the results got by greedy algorithms may be far from the optimal assignments.

3   Stable Matching Scheduler

Multi-programmed workloads consist of multiple independent applications that run together. When multi-programmed workloads are running on single-ISA HMPs, a fundamental problem is how to schedule applications to appropriate cores. In this section we propose a novel scheduler based on the matching game theory. To facilitate the discussion, we suppose a one-to-one mapping in our stable matching scheduler where the numbers of applications and cores are equal. However, the proposed scheduler can also deal with the multiple-to-one mapping problem by set a quota of applications for each core, as in the well-known college admission model [15].

3.1   Scheduler Algorithm

In the single-ISA HMPs, due to the heterogeneity of cores and the diverse resource demands of applications, it is likely that different applications/cores would prefer different cores/applications. Further more, the preferences of single application or core would vary across phases [1]. Therefore, to improve the efficiency of scheduling, one must take the diverse preferences of applications and cores into account. In this paper, we treat each application and core as distinct individuals with their own preferences. To solve the matching problem between applications and cores, we modify the marriage model to fit the circumstances of scheduling problem.

Algorithm 1. Stable scheduling algorithm.

Require: *the preference structure*
Ensure: *a stable matching*;
 1: **for** *i*in1...*N* **do**
 2:     %*initialize two arrays AppPartner, CorePartner*
 3:     AppPartner[app_i] = **0**; CorePartner[$core_i$] = **0**
 4: **end for**
 5: **while true do**
 6:     **if** no app_i exists such that AppPartner[app_i] == **0 then**
 7:         **return**
 8:     **end if**
 9:     select app_i such that AppPartner[app_i]== **0** randomly
10:     select $core_j$ as the first core on app_i's preference list whom app_i have not been yet proposed to
11:     **if** CorePartner[$core_j$]== **0 then**
12:         CorePartner[$core_j$] ← app_i; AppPartner[app_i] ← $core_j$
13:     **else if** app_i is higher than CorePartner[$core_j$] on $core_j$ preference list **then**
14:         AppPartner[CorePartner[$core_j$]] ← **0**
15:         CorePartner[$core_j$] ← app_i; AppPartner[app_i] ← $core_j$
16:     **end if**
17: **end while**

The basis assumptions of stable scheduling algorithm are defined as follows. Given two sets of Apps and Cores with equal size. Each individual in the set Apps/Cores has a preference lists Papp/Pcore on the opposite set Cores/Apps. The set Apps and Cores together with their preference lists are called a preference structure. AppPartner and CorePartner are used to record the current matching state of each application and core. A matching is called stable when there does not exist any alternative application-core partners (appi, corej) in which both appi and corej prefer each other rather than the individual to which they are currently matched. Based on the above assumptions, Algorithm 1 illustrates the detail steps of the stable scheduling algorithm. It takes the preference structure as input and outputs a stable matching at last. It has been proved that this algorithm can always lead to a stable matching in $O(n^2)$ iterations.

A simple example about how the proposed stable matching algorithm works is shown below. Consider a scenario where four applications are running on a system consisting of four different cores. Suppose that each application exhibits IPC on each core reported in Table 1a. From these data, we could infer the preference lists for applications and cores respectively, as shown in Tables 1b and 1c.

Table 1. Preference lists of applications and cores

(a) IPC of each application

	core1	core2	core3	core4
app1	1.8	1.5	1.2	1.1
app2	1.3	1.2	0.9	0.8
app3	1.0	1.3	1.5	1.2
app4	1.5	1.1	1.3	1.0

(b) The app's preferences

App	1st	2nd	3rd	4th
app1	core1	core2	core3	core4
app2	core1	core2	core3	core4
app3	core3	core2	core4	core1
app4	core1	core3	core2	core4

(c) The core's preferences

Core	1st	2nd	3rd	4th
core1	app1	app4	app2	app3
core2	app1	app3	app2	app4
core3	app3	app4	app1	app2
core4	app3	app1	app4	app2

Figure 1 shows the procedure of matching process. In the first round, all applications propose to their favorite cores. core1 receives three proposals from app1, app2 and app4. core3 receives proposal from app3. Then core1 accepts the best proposal app1 and reject the others. core3 would directly accept app3 as its partner. The first round ends up with (app1,core1), (app3,core3). In the second round, app2 and app4 which were rejected in the first round propose to their second choices respectively. core2 accepts the proposal of app2, while core3 compares the new proposal from app4 with its current partner app3 and decides to remain unchange. The second round ends

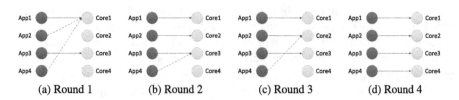

(a) Round 1   (b) Round 2   (c) Round 3   (d) Round 4

Fig. 1. An example of stable matching

up with (app1,core1), (app2,core2), (app3,core3). The whole process proceeds until every application finds a partner in the round 4, and finally reports a stable matching (app1,core1), (app2,core2), (app3,core3), (app4,core4). This assignment reports a total IPC of 5.5, which equals to the optimal result found by the exhaustive searching algorithm.

Table 2. Application characteristics

Characteristics	Description
System call	System calls
Memory read	Instructions which read from memory
Memory write	Instructions which write to memory
Taken Branches	Token conditional branches
Control	Control instructions
Interger	Integer instructions
Floating-point	Floating-point instructions
SSE	SIMD Extensions instructions
Other insts	Other instructions
Register traffic	Average register operands
Float register traffic	Average float register operands
Memory temporal locality	Average re-use distance for 64B cache blocks
Instruction level parallelism	Instructions between producer and consumer instructions

3.2 Predction Model

The stable matching scheduler treats both applications and cores as individuals with their own preferences. In order to infer those preferences, we need to predict the performance of each application on different cores in runtime. As mentioned in Sect. 2, we construct an ANN prediction model with the architecture independent characteristics. The used architecture independent application characteristics are shown in Table 2. Collecting these application characteristics needs hardware performance counters supporting. Fortunately, such counters are already widely used in modern processors for operating system management, error diagnosis, code optimization and scheduling. Most of th required characteristics can be directly collected by existing performance counters [18, 21, 23–25]. And the rest memory temporal locality and instruction level parallelism information can also be measured by the methods proposed in previous papers [18, 21].

As illustrated in Fig. 2, the ANN models are firstly trained off-line, and then used on-line. In the training stage, to collect enough application characteristics, we selected 19 representative benchmarks (perlbench, bzip2, gcc, bwaves, mcf, milc, leslie3d, namd, gobmk, soplex, hmmer, GemsFDTD, libquantum, h264ref, lbm, omnetpp, astar, sphinx3) from SPEC CPU2006 benchmark suite [17] compiled as X86-ISA binary with train input dataset and break each application as 200 sample phases. A sampling phase is consisted by a fixed number of instructions, such as 10 million instructions per phase.

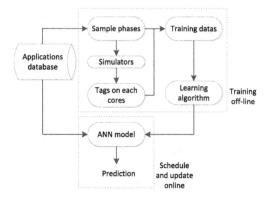

Fig. 2. ANN model training

All the sample phases are executed on simulator, and the corresponding tags (i.e., performance or energy efficiency) are recorded. We randomly divide all the data into training set and test set, then we train the ANN models for each core. According to our experiment results, the average absolute prediction error of training algorithm is 9.73 % on test data. As a comparison, we also implemented one of the state-of-the-art work PIE (performance impact estimation) prediction model [21] under the same experimental environment, and PIE model only reaches 13.60 % of the average absolute prediction error. After the training, the ANN models are used in scheduling to predict the performanc of application each application on different cores online.

4   Experiments and Results

In this section we describe our experimental methodology and discuss the results.

4.1   Experimental Methodology

This section describes the experimental methodology we used for evaluating our stable matching scheduler. As shown in [10], the best way to design a single-ISA HMP for a variety of multi-programmed workloads is by customizing cores to subsets of workloads and there is no typically monotonic relationship among cores for different applications. In the experiments, we consider eight cores with different numbers of issue widths, L1 cache sizes, frequencies, and other crucial micro-architecture features as listed in Table 3. Those cores span a wide spectrum of heterogeneities that may meet the diverse architecture demands of applications. We consider three hypothesis single-ISA HMPs with 4-core (core2, core3, core4, core5), 6-core (core1 - core6) and 8-core (core1 - core8) using different combination of these defined cores. We simulate these single-ISA HMPs with the gem5 [26] cycle-accurate simulator in syscall emulation mode. Power is estimated with McPAT models [27]. We collect the application characteristics with MICA [22], a Pin tool which allows us to collect a number of architecture independent application characteristics.

Table 3. Core configurations

Cores	Width	ROB	Frequency	Float/Int Register	L1 cache
core1	2	32	1G Hz	64/64	32 KB 4-way
core2	2	64	1G Hz	128/128	16 KB 4-way
core3	4	64	1G Hz	64/64	32 KB 4-way
core4	4	96	1G Hz	128/128	16 KB 4-way
core5	6	96	1G Hz	64/64	32 KB 4-way
core6	6	128	1G Hz	128/128	16 KB 4-way
core7	8	128	2G Hz	64/64	32 KB 4-way
core8	8	196	2G Hz	128/128	16 KB 4-way

To evaluate the proposed stable matching scheduler with diverse applications, we selected 12 representative benchmarks from the SPEC CPU2006 benchmarks: four integer benchmarks (perlbench, bzip2, h264ref, hmmer, libquantum) and eight floating point benchmarks (milc, leslie3d, namd, soplex, GemsFDTD, lbm, sphinx3). From another perspective, six of them (bzip2, libquantum, GemsFDTD, milc, leslie3d, soplex) are memory-intensive applications and the rest (perlbench, h264ref, hmmer, namd, lbm, sphinx3) are compute-intensive applications. In order to schedule the applications with different phases with the sample in the ANN model training stage, all these benchmarks use the test dataset as input. We randomly mixed the above 12 benchmarks to compose the multi-programmed workloads. For each HMPs configuration (4-core, 6-core, 8-core), 20 different multi-programmed workloads are executed, we report the finally average results.

In general, the interaction between cores would affect the overall performance of system. In this paper, the workloads are all composed by independent applications, which have limited and symmetric impact on each other. To focus on the studying of scheduling, we neglect the effect of interaction between applications by making the same assumption as previous proposals [8, 9, 14] that L2 cache and off-chip memory bandwidth is statically partitioned among the cores.

The frequent migration of applications between cores would also incur performance overhead, which mainly comes from the context switch and cache warmup effects. Previous related proposals [9, 11, 21, 28] have quantified the migration overhead at different time intervals (a continuous time slice). Usually, for a 2.5 ms migration frequency, the performance overhead due to migration is negligible, less than 1 %. Based on their researches, we assume a 10 ms scheduling time interval[1], where the performance overhead is nearly 1 %. Further more, to avoid the unnecessary migrations, we could take the affinity of current matched applications and cores into consideration when generating the preference lists (i.e.,give the current partner a higher weight).

The stable matching scheduler makes scheduling decision before entering each time interval. The overhead of the stable matching scheduler mainly comes from the

---

[1] A time interval contains unfixed number of instructions, which is different with definition of sampling phase in the ANN training stage. Scheduling by time interval promises us to schedule different phases with the sample in the offline training.

performance prediction and the scheduling algorithms. We discuss the two parts overhead respectively.

To reduce the total time overhead, we propose to implement the most time-consuming ANN model in a low overhead hardware. To be specific, the hardware ANN model is consist of an input layer, a hidden layer, and an output layer. The input layer has 13 neurons, corresponding to the 13 application characteristics. The hidden layer has 10 neurons, which are fully connected with the neurons of input layer. The synapsis between each pair of neurons corresponds to a weight. The output layer has 1 neurons, which is fully connected with the neurons in hidden layer. In the implementation of the ANN model, all neurons and synapsis are expressed by 32-bit fixed-point numbers. As a result, we need $768 = (13 + 10 + 1) \times 32$ bit registers to store all neurons, and need $4480 \times N = (13 \times 10 + 10 \times 1) \times 32 \times N$ bit SRAM to store the weights (all the weights can be set off-line or updated on-line), where N is the number of processors in the HMPs system[2]. For a HMPs system with 8 processors, it only needs a 4.38 KB SRAM to store all weights. Besides the storage cost, the hardware ANN model also needs (13 $\times$ 10 + 10 $\times$ 1) 32-bit multipliers, (12 + 9) 32-bit adders, and (10 + 1) linear inter-polation units[3]. To evaluate the overall area and power cost of the hardware ANN model, we have done the synthesis of ANN model using Synopsys tools. The main power/area breakdown by component type are shown in Table 4. The hardware ANN model allows us to progress the prediction in parallel with the application execution, overlapping the delay of prediction.

Table 4. The area and power cost of the hardware ANN model

Component	Area(mm^2)	Power(mW)
Total	0.144313	8.0934
Memory	0.098881	1.2283
Combinational	0.010896	1.6101
Clock_network	0.008252	1.7289
Register	0.026284	3.5261

The scheduling algorithm would be executed on the biggest core in a HMPs system. After the prediction, the chosen core invokes the stable matching algorithm to get the assignment. We execute the stable matching algorithm on core8 to estimate the time overhead. The time overhead is related with the problem size. And it averagely takes 500 cycles for a 4-core system, 1200 cycles for a 6-core system and 3000 cycles for a 8-core system. Taking this overhead into consideration, we assume 5000 cycles, which is negligible for the 10 ms scheduling interval, for the core executing the scheduling algorithm to make scheduling decision at the end of each interval, it does not neces-sarily influence the execution of other cores.

---

[2] Since all Processors in the HMPs system may have different microarchitectures, we need N different sets of weights.

[3] The linea interpolation units are leveraged to approximately calculate the outputs of active function (e.g. sigmoid or tanh).

4.2   Results and Analysis

In this section, we present the performance and energy efficiency results of our scheduler. For comparison, we also evaluate the random scheduler [6], the round robin scheduler [6, 11], the sampling-based scheduler [7] and the greedy scheduler [12, 14] in our experimental environment.

First, we target to optimize the overall performance of system. The global BIPS (billions instructions per second), defined as the ratio between the total instruction count and the execution time, is used as metric to evaluate the overall system performance.

Figure 3 provides us an example of 4 applications (libquantum, lbm, GemsFDTD, bzip2) running in the 4-core system with the scheduling details of different schedulers.

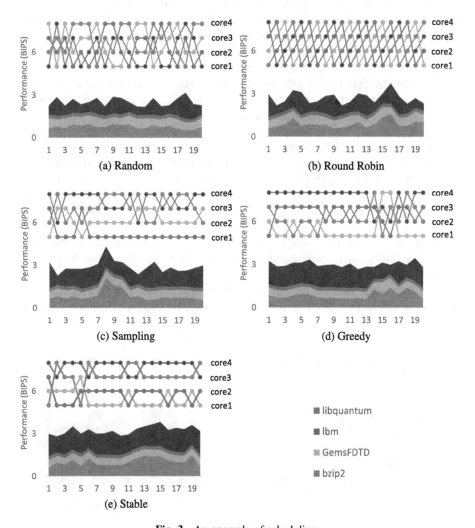

Fig. 3. An example of scheduling

The upper portion of each subgraph shows the migration trajectory of the applications. The area chart in each subgraph indicates the correspond performance of the applications in every interval.

The random scheduler assigns applications on cores randomly in each time interval, such scheduling is not likely to find the optimal assignment. The random scheduler has the worst average performance of 2.52 BIPS. The round robin scheduler ensures different cores are equally shared among the applications, it usually presents a slight performance improvement over random scheduler. The round robin scheduler reports average performance of 2.72 BIPS. The sampling-based scheduler exhaustively searches all 4! = 24 the possible assignments and employs the best assignment. The sampling-based scheduler finally achieves 2.90 BIPS, better than both the random scheduler and the round robin scheduler. The previous greedy algorithm VarF&AppIPC [12, 14] is specially designed for system that frequency is the only heterogeneity between cores. We modify a version of VarF&AppIPC to apply the greedy algorithm in our experimental environment. The applications are sorted by the prediction performance, and the cores are sorted by their areas. Then applications are assigned to cores according to their corresponding positions in rankings. Though the greedy scheduler may lead to suboptimal assignments, it avoids the bad assignments and the sampling overhead. As a result, the greedy scheduler achieves better performance (average 3.01 BIPS) than the sampling-based scheduler.

Finally, the proposed stable matching scheduler achieved the best performance improvement of 3.24 BIPS among all 5 schedulers. From this subgraph we can infer that the application libquantum and core4 prefers each other in most intervals. The similar situation also happened between the application bzip2 and core3, lbm and core2, GemsFDTD and core1. However, the opposite was also true in some intervals. The stable matching scheduler catches this variation and makes the best scheduling decisions.

Figure 4a reports the average results of 20 different workloads on the three single-ISA HMPs. Similar with the above example, the round robin scheduler presents slight performance improvement over the random scheduler by 9.15 % (4-core), 6.63 % (6-core) and 4.45 % (8-core) respectively. The sampling-based scheduler compares to the random scheduler with the performance improvement of 15.41 % (4-core), 2.94 %

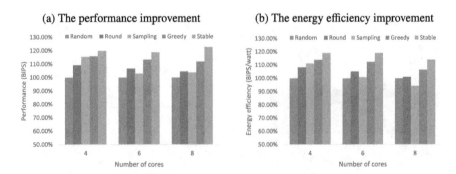

Fig. 4. The average scheduling results

(6-core) and 3.76 % (8-core). The efficiency of sampling-based scheduler decreases rapidly as the possible assignments increasing with the core number, up to 40320 assignment candidates with 8 cores, it is almost impossible to examine all the assignments to find the optimal one. Thus we evaluate the sampling-based scheduler on 6-core and 8-core system through sampling only a subset of possible assignments and select the best sampled one. Even though, the sampling overhead is still remarkable. The experimental results well comply with the intuition that the sampling-based scheduler is inappropriate for large-scale system. The greedy scheduler outperforms the random scheduler by 15.73 % (4-core), 13.32 % (6-core) and 11.93 % (8-core). Such results suggest that the greedy scheduler exhibits worse performance on system with larger number of cores. It is because the greedy algorithm has the greater possibility to make local optimal decision in a larger space of possible assignments. The stable matching scheduler achieves the best performance among all schedulers, outperforming random scheduler by 19.86 % (4-core), 18.78 % (6-core) and 22.78 % (8-core), respectively. Even comparing with the greedy scheduler, the stable matching scheduler reports performance improvement by 3.8 % (4-core), 4.9 % (6-core) and 9.7 % (8-core). It is worth noting that the stable matching scheduler is almost not affected by the number of cores in the system, indicating both better efficiency and scalability.

The BIPS is actually a performance-only metric. We also evaluated the proposed schedulers with the energy efficiency metric that combines both performance and power consideration together. Energy efficiency is measured by the ratio between the global BIPS and power. The average energy efficiency results are reported in Fig. 4b. The stable matching scheduler still achieves the best energy efficiency among all 5 schedulers, outperforming the random scheduler 19.10 % (4-core), 19.08 % (6-core) and 13.98 % (8-core), respectively. Comparing with the greedy scheduler, the stable matching scheduler reports energy efficiency improvement by 4.7 % (4-core), 5.9 % (6-core) and 7.3 % (8-core).

5 Conclusion and FutureWork

In this paper we propose a novel stable matching scheduler to meet the scheduling problem caused by the increasing diversity of application-specific heterogeneity in HMPs. In the proposed scheduler, applications and cores are regarded as two sets of individuals with their own preferences, and the scheduler can always lead to a stable matching between the two sets. According to our experiments, the proposed stable matching scheduler averagely improves the performance against the random scheduler by 19.86 % (4-core), 18.78 % (6-core), 22.78 % (8-core), respectively. Moreover, as the continuous increasing of the scale of HMPs, the proposed stable matching scheduler will further improve the efficiency of application scheduling. In this paper we consider the scheduling of multi-programmed workloads. Single (or a combination of) multi-threaded applications is another common scenario in HMPs. For the scheduling of multi-threaded applications, it also requires that the scheduler identifies the bottleneck thread(s) and ensures such threads to be accelerated on big cores. We could take such priority of bottleneck threads into consideration in our future stable matching scheduler.

References

1. Sherwood, T., Sair, S., Calder, B.: Phase tracking and prediction. In: the 30th Annual International Symposium on Computer Architecture (ISCA2003), pp. 336–347. ACM, New York (2003)
2. big.LITTLE processing with ARM Cortex-A15 & Cortex-A7: Improving energy efficiency in high-performance mobile paltform. http://www.arm.com/files/downloads/big_LITTLE_Final_Final.pdf
3. Variable SMP a multi-core CPU architecture for low power and high performance. http://www.nvidia.com/content/PDF/tegra_white_papers/Variable-SMP-A-Multi-Core-CPU-Architecture-for-Low-Power-and-High-Performance-v1.1.pdf
4. The future is fusion: The industry-changing impact of accelerated computing. http://sites.amd.com/us/Documents/AMD_fusion_Whitepaper.pdf
5. Kahle, J.A., Day, M.N., Hofstee, H.P., Johns, C.R., Maeurer, T.R., Shippy, D.: Introduction to the cell multiprocessor. IBM J. Res. Dev. - POWER5 Packag. Arch. **49**(4), 589–604 (2005). IBM Corp, Riverton
6. Marco, C., Faniel, P.B.: Understanding the Linux Kernel. O'Reilly Media, Sebastopol (2002)
7. Kumar, R., Tullsen, D.M., Ranganathan, P., Jouppi, N.P., Farkas, K.I.: Single-ISA heterogeneous multi-core architectures for multithreaded workload performance. In: the 31th Annual International Symposium on Computer Architecture (ISCA2004), pp. 64–75. ACM, New York (2004)
8. Ghiasi, S., Keller, T., Rawson, F.: Scheduling for heterogeneous processors in server systems. In: the 2nd Conference on Computing Frontiers (CF2005), pp.199–210. ACM, New York (2005)
9. Becchi, M., Crowley, P.: Dynamic thread assignment on heterogeneous multiprocessor architectures. In: The 3rd Conference on Computing Frontiers (CF2006), pp. 29–40. ACM, New York (2006)
10. Kumar, R., Tullsen, D.M., Jouppi, N.P.: Core architecture optimization for heterogeneous chip multiprocessors. In: The 15th International Conference on Parallel Architectures and Compilation Techniques (PACT2006), pp. 23–32. ACM, New York (2006)
11. Rangan, K., Powell, M.D., Wei, G., Brooks, D.: Achieving uniform performance and maximizing throughput in the presence of heterogeneity. In: The 17th International Symposium on High-Performance Computer Architecture (HPCA2011), pp. 3–14. IEEE, San Antonio (2011)
12. Teodorescu, R., Torrellas, J.: Variation-aware application scheduling and power management for chip multiprocessors. In: The 35th Annual International Symposium on Computer Architecture (ISCA2008), pp. 363–374. IEEE, Beijing (2008)
13. Koufaty, D., Reddy, D., Hahn, S.: Bias scheduling in heterogeneous multi-core architectures. In: The 5th European Conference on Computer Systems, pp. 125–138. ACM, New York (2010)
14. Winter, J.A., Albonesi, D.H., Shoemaker, C.A.: Scalable thread scheduling and global power management for heterogeneous many-core architectures. In: the 19th International Conference on Parallel Architectures and Compilation Techniques (PACT2010), pp. 29–40. ACM, New York (2010)
15. Gale, D., Shapley, L.S.: College admissions and the stability of marriage. Am. Math. Mon. **69**, 9–15 (1962)
16. Stable matching: theory, evidence, and practical design. http://www.nobelprize.org/nobel_prizes/economic-sciences/laureates/2012/popular-economicsciences2012.pdf

17. Henning, J.L.: SPEC CPU2006 benchmark descriptions. ACM SIGARCH Comput. Archit. News **34**(4), 1–17 (2006). ACM, New York

18. Weidan, W., Benjamin, C.L.: Inferred models for dynamic and sparse hardware-software spaces. In: The 45th Annual IEEE/ACM International Symposium on Microarchitecture (Micro2012), pp. 413–424. IEEE, Washington (2012)

19. Shelepov, D., Saez Alcaide, J.C., Jeffery, S., Fedorova, A., Perez, N., Huang, Z.F., Blagodurov, S., Kumar, V.: HASS: a scheduler for heterogeneous multicore systems. ACM SIGOPS Operating Syst. Rev. **43**(2), 66–75 (2009). ACM, New York

20. Shouqing, H., Qi, L., Longbing, Z., Jian, W.: Processes scheduling on heterogeneous multicore architecture with hardware support. In: The 6th International Conference on Networking, Architecture and Storage (NAS2011), pp. 236–241. IEEE, Dalian (2011)

21. Van, C.K., Jaleel, A., Eeckhout, L., Narvaez, P., Emer, J.: Scheduling heterogeneous multicores through performance impact estimation (PIE). In: the 39th Annual International Symposium on Computer Architecture (ISCA2012), pp. 213–224. IEEE, Portland (2012)

22. Kenneth, H., Lieven, E.: Microarchitecture-independent workload characterization. IEEE Micro Hot Tutirials **27**(3), 63–72 (2007). IEEE

23. Eranian, S.: Perfmon2: a flexible performance monitoring interface for Linux. In: Ottawa Linux Symposium Proceedings, pp.269–288 (2006)

24. Suh, G.E., Devadas, S., Rudolph, L.: A new memory monitoring scheme for memory-aware scheduling and partitioning. In: the 18th International Symposium on High-Performance Computer Architecture (HPCA2002), pp. 117–128. IEEE, Boston (2002)

25. Mericas, A.: Performance monitoring on the POWER5 microprocessor. In: John, L.K., Eeckhout, L. (eds.) Performance Evaluation and Benchmarking, pp.247–266. CRC Press, Boca Raton (2005)

26. Binkert, N., Beckmann, B., Black, G., et al.: The gem5 simulator. ACM SIGARCH Comput. Archit. News **39**(2), 1–7 (2011). ACM, New York

27. Li, S., Ahn, J.H., Strong, R.D., Brockman, J.B., Tullsen, D.M., Jouppi, N.P.: McPAT: an integrated power, area, and timing modeling framework for multicore and manycore architectures. In: the 42th Annual IEEE/ACM International Symposium on Microarchitecture (Micro2009), pp. 469–480. IEEE, New York (2009)

28. Powell, M.D., Biswas, A., Gupta, S., Mukherjee, S.: Architectural core salvaging in a multicore processor for hard-error tolerance. ACM SIGARCH Computer Architecture News **37**(3), 93–104 (2009). ACM, New York

RPECA-Rumor Propagation Based Eventual Consistency Assessment Algorithm

Dong Zhang[1,2], Zhiyuan Su[1,2(✉)], Kaiyuan Qi[1,2], Guomao Xin[1,2], and Peng Wei[1,2]

[1] State Key Laboratory of High-End Server and Storage Technology, Jinan 250101, China
[2] Inspur Electronic Information Industry Co., Ltd., Jinan 250101, China
{zhangdong, suzhiyuan, qiky, xingm, weip}@inspur.com

Abstract. Replicating data across servers or storages in different data centers allows using data closer to the client and reducing latency for applications, In addition, it also increases the availability in the event of one or some datacenters failure. Hence, replica consistency among all nodes is a major consideration when designing high-availability across-domain datacenters. Even lots of mechanisms are proposed to reach this consistency target, we believe knowing the degree of consistency is helpful to an application developer as the dimension of uncertainty is reduced: The quality of service (QoS) becomes, to some degree, predictable. For this purpose, this paper proposes a novel algorithm called RPECA which can be applied to monitor consistency behaviors in a cost-efficient way. RPECA is based on theory of rumor propagation in complex networks. In this paper, we focus on the probability of each node's specific status in the network (Ignorant, Spreader or Stifler). Based on the discrete-time markov chain model technique, we apply a set of topology-independent equations to describe the microscope dynamic property of each node at any given time. Besides, we construct the whole phase diagram of the rumor spreading process in SF and small-world networks to simulate consistency behavior. In the experimental part, on one hand, the numerical results of our RPECA method could almost coincide with the empirical results of Monte Carlo (MC) simulations, which proves that our algorithm could simulated the whole phase diagram correctly. On the other hand, since the numerical results could be solved with less iterations, our RPECA algorithm could significantly outperform MC method with respect to time complexity.

Keywords: Eventually consistency · Rumor propagation · Markov chain · Across-datacenter

1 Introduction

Over the last few years, massive data has been generated by the huge and constantly-growing number of smart phones, wearable devices, sensors and social network users. In order to deal with the big data problem, data centers are becoming significantly important. Computing terminals, like PC, mobile devices, usually access these data stored on a server in data center. To accommodate the fast growth of data

© Springer International Publishing Switzerland 2015
Y. Chen et al. (Eds.): APPT 2015, LNCS 9231, pp. 60–72, 2015.
DOI: 10.1007/978-3-319-23216-4_5

centers and servers, data or its fragments are distributed and replicated across a subset of nodes such that the system can tolerate a wide range of network, power, and/or other type of failures that could put off-line large quantities of data. For example, Google's e-mail service, Gmail, synchronously replicates across five data centers to sustain two data center outages: one planned and one unplanned.

The term "eventual consistency" implies not only how fast all updates of data are complete but also that updates of data are successfully executed on all of their distributed replicas. Models designed to reach "eventual consistency" among servers in one data center or in multiple data centers varies from each other, but most of them are with respect to "messaging mechanism" or "propagating mechanism" (Fig. 1). Intuitively speaking, when an update of one piece of data on a node occurs, the node will propagate this message to other replicas ASAP so that they can be updated to the latest state. Unfortunately, due to the network latency, outage of server, data loss, single failure or other reasons, this propagation process is not always successfully carried out as expectation. To the best of our knowledge, there is little efforts made to detect how these "random noise" affects the performance of "eventual consistency" model. Concretely, how much percentage of nodes that are updated successfully after one round propagation, which nodes are updated and which nodes are not, how much time do we need to get "eventual consistency" and whether the network topology among replica nodes affects the performance. We believe that answers to these questions are critical for building a reliable "eventual consistency" model.

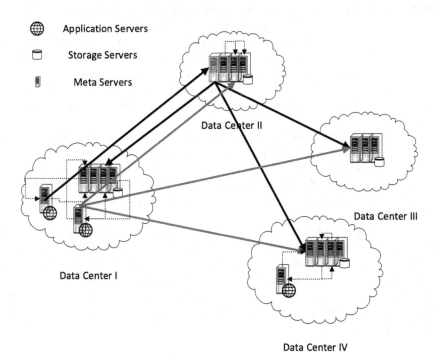

Fig. 1. Messaging mechanism for eventually consistency in multiple data centers and in one data center

We found that the process of rumor propagation are much similar with the message propagation mechanism in eventually consistency under the three respects (1) Both of them are based on propagation process; (2) When a node are receiving a message, its state will be updated and then propagated to its neighbors; (3) The propagation process will be interrupted or failed by some "random noise", which means in each step of propagation, there is a probability of success. These observations motivated us to develop a novel rumor propagation based eventually consistency assessment algorithm (RPECA). To the best of our knowledge, RPECA is the first to promote the rumor propagation mechanism on evaluating the degree of eventually consistency.

The rest of paper are organized as follows: Sect. 2 described the related work about rumor propagation and eventually consistency. Sect. 3 proposed a new rumor propagation model for eventually consistency assessment, including the hypothesis and the math which is how we compute the final percentage of updated nodes after one round propagation. Sect. 4 gives the experimental results on Monte Carlo (MC) simulations and the numerical solutions of our assessment algorithm.

2 Related Work

2.1 Eventual Consistency

The CAP theorem [1] shows that for any given pair of request the write is followed by read, the distributed system can guarantee only 2 out of the following three attributes: consistency, availability and partition tolerance. PACELC [2] further interprets CAP, which claims two tradeoffs, including consistency & availability and consistency & latency. Eventual consistency across the literature uses a variety of techniques to propagate updates (e.g. general causally-ordered broadcast [3], or pairwise anti-entropy [4]). For a general high-level comparison of our work with various notions of eventual consistency appearing in the literature, we refer to the literatures on the assessment of consistency behavior.

Bailis et al. [5] introduced Probabilistically Bounded Staleness (PBS) into modeling the expected staleness of data returned by eventually consistent quorum-replicated data stores and developed the WARS latency model to explain how message reordering leads to staleness under Dynamo-style quorum systems. Their approach is limited to the usual bounds of simulation precision but gives a more cost-effective method for studying consistency behavior.

Zellag and Kemme [6] proposed a generalized approach for detecting consistency anomalies for arbitrary cloud applications accessing various types of cloud data stores in transactional or non-transactional contexts and verified the effectiveness under Google App Engine and Cassandra data stores. At runtime, their approach builds a dependency graph to detect cycles, i.e., consistency violations. To the best of our knowledge, their approach is currently limited to storage systems offering at least Causal Consistency [7].

Muntasir et al. [8] think that a consistency benchmark should paint a comprehensive picture of the relationship between the storage system under the workload, the pattern of failures, and the consistency observed by client. Hence, they presented a client-centric benchmarking methodology for understanding eventual consistency in distributed key-value storage systems. Without injecting operations into the workload, they extends the popular YCSB benchmark to measure the staleness of data returned by reads using the concept of Δ-atomicity [9].

As far as we know, little publications on consistency monitoring exist. All consistency benchmarking approaches might also be candidates for consistency monitoring but are currently too expensive to run continuously. We believe that our rumor propagation based eventual consistency assessment method could be a meaningful try on this field.

2.2 Rumor Propagation and Complex Network

Since Erdos and Renyi proposed ER random network at 1960 [10], complex network has been widely studied and many kinds of complex networks were proposed, such as WS small-world network [11], NW small-world network [12] and scale-free (SF) network [13]. It turns out that Internet [14], WWW and other social, technological and biological networks [15] are all proved to be heterogeneous network and could be categorized into SF networks. In these SF networks, the probability distribution that a given node being connected to k other nodes follows power law distribution $P(k) \sim k^{-\gamma}$, with the remarkable feature that $\gamma \leq 3$.

One of the important problems on different complex networks is how to model the process of rumor spreading. It has been intensively studied for many years. The main approach for solving this problem is the Mean-Field (MF) approximation. [16–20]. MF approaches suppose that all nodes in a degree class have the same dynamical properties and neglect the fluctuation of nodes.

M. Nekovee and Y. Moreno also introduced a stochastic model for the spread of rumors, and derive mean-field equations describing the dynamics of rumor propagation model on complex social networks [24].

MF approaches are extremely useful to assess the critical properties of rumor or epidemic spreading models. However, they are not designed to consider the states of individual node. S. Gomez and A. ARENAS proposed a Markov chain approach [22, 23] to address epidemic problem on different SF networks for a SIS model [21], which considers the probability of a given node being infected or susceptible. However, they did not consider a common situation called SIR model in epidemic or rumor spreading models, in which a node would never spread the epidemic or rumor anymore which is called being in a stifler states (SIR model).

In the following section, we would like to introduce the SIR model into simulating consistency behavior and formulate this SIR model based on some reasonable hypothesis.

3 Hypothesis and Math

In this section, we first proposed a new model of rumor spreading on replicas-network. The replicas-network topology could be complicated based on the geographical position and the link relationship. Therefore, we model this process in two different representative complex networks, small world network and scale free (SF) network, which describe the most two typical network topologies. Compared with previous models, RPECA provides a fine-grained description of this spreading process. Firstly, we originally introduce the susceptible-infected-removed (SIR) model on epidemics [26] into the MK model [25] on rumor propagation. Secondly, we describe three formulations of rumor spreading with SIR form based on probabilistic discrete-time Markov chains and apply them to both weighted and un-weighted networks.

As we discussed in Part I and Part II, our RPECA is defined in the following way. We consider a replica-network including N nodes which are subdivided into ignorant, spreader and stifler nodes corresponding to the rumor spreading process. Ignorants are those nodes who have not heard the rumor and hence they are susceptible to be informed. In the replica-network scenario, it means the node that are not updated to the newest state. Spreaders are defined as the nodes that have heard the rumor and try to spread it, corresponding to the nodes that have been successfully updated to the newest state and keep sending this messages to its neighbors. At last, stiflers are those who know the rumor but not spread any longer, which corresponding to the nodes that are in the newest state but not sending "updating messages" any more in a replica-network scenario. The system will be converged when there is no spreaders. Therefore, the rate of stifler after the one round "updating messages" could be used as a way to assess the degree of consistency.

Based on MK [25] model, the spreading process is launched by spreaders. Spreaders try to send "updating requests" to their neighbors. The spreading procedure are governed by the following set rules

(1) A spreader makes a number μ of trials to transmit the rumor (updating requests) to its neighbors.
(2) Whenever a spreader contacts an ignorant, the ignorant becomes a spreader at a probability λ.
(3) When a spreader contacts another spreader or a stifler the initiating spreader becomes a stifler at a rate α.

We assume that whenever a node becomes a stifler, it never becomes an ignorant again.

Now let us consider the probability that any given node v is at one specific state (Ignorant, Spreader or Stifler) when the spreading process is stable. We denote the matrix A with entries $\{a_{ij}\}$ as the $N - by - N$ adjacent matrix of the network. In addition, the network is weighted in most cases. Hence, let $\{w_{ij}\}$ denote the weights of the connections between nodes, and $w_i = \sum_j w_{ij}$ is the total strength of node i [18]. Last but not least, entries $\{r_{ij}\}$ represents the probability that any given node i is in contact with a node j, which generates a matrix R. These entries represent the probabilities that existing links in the network are used to transmit the rumor. Apparently, if $a_{ij} = 0$, then $r_{ij} = 0$.

Let $I^v(t)$, $S^v(t)$ and $R^v(t)$ represent the probability of a node v being in the ignorant, spreader and stifler state at time t respectively. These variables satisfy the normalization condition $I^v(t) + S^v(t) + R^v(t) = 1$. $q_v^{ii}(t)$ is the probability of node v not being infected to be a spreader. Obviously, the probability that it makes a transition to the spreader could be denoted with $q_v^{is}(t) = 1 - q_v^{ii}(t)$. It then follows that

$$q_v^{ii}(t) = \prod_j^N (1 - \lambda r_{jv} S_j(t)) \tag{1}$$

where $S_j(t)$ is the probability that a node j is in spreader state at time t. Hence the discrete-time version of the evolution of the probability of a node v being in ignorant state reads

$$I^v(t+1) = I^v(t) \times q_v^{ii}(t) \tag{2}$$

Similarly, we could obtain the probability that a spreader node not being influenced at time t and still is in spreader state. Let $q_v^{ss}(t)$ denote this probability, where

$$q_v^{ss}(t) = \prod_j^N (1 - \alpha r_{jv}(S_j(t) + R_j(t))) \tag{3}$$

Accordingly, we obtain $q_v^{sr}(t) = 1 - q_v^{ss}(t)$, where $q_v^{sr}(t)$ represents the probability of node v becoming from spreader to stifler. Based on the discrete-time markov chain model, we could get the corresponding version on the evolution of a node v being in spreader and stifler state as follows.

$$S^v(t+1) = I^v(t) \times q_v^{is}(t) + S^v(t) \times q_v^{ss}(t) \tag{4}$$

$$R^v(t+1) = R^v(t) + S^v(t) \times q_v^{sr}(t) \tag{5}$$

Apparently, $I^v(t+1) + S^v(t+1) + R^v(t+1) = 1$ and these formulations (2), (4), (5) depend on the assumption that the probabilities of a node being in a special state at time t are independent random variables [22]. This hypothesis is proved to be correct in most of the complex networks based on in-persistence of dynamical correlations. Therefore, inserting Eqs. (1) and (3) into Eqs. (2), (4) and (5), we get the rumor spreading equations as

$$I^v(t+1) = I^v(t)[\prod_j^N (1 - \lambda r_{jv} S_j(t))] \tag{6}$$

$$S^v(t+1) = I^v(t)[1 - \prod_{j}^{N}(1 - \lambda r_{jv}S_j(t))] + S^v(t)[\prod_{j}^{N}(1 - \alpha r_{jv}(S_j(t) + R_j(t)))] \quad (7)$$

$$R^v(t+1) = R^v(t) + S^v(t)[1 - \prod_{j}^{N}(1 - \alpha r_{jv}(S_j(t) + R_j(t)))] \quad (8)$$

Now we consider how to compute the contact probability r_{ij}. As mentioned above, without loss of generality, a number μ of transitions from a spreader to its neighbors can be seen as μ random walkers leaving node i at each time step. If all neighbors are contacted in one time step, μ could be set the limit $\mu \to \infty$ and $r_{ij} = a_{ij}$ no matter whether the network is weighted. If not, then we could get

$$r_{ij} = 1 - (1 - \frac{w_{ij}}{w_i})^\mu \quad (9)$$

Now we can get the phase diagram of every kind of network solving the system formed by Eqs. (6, 7, and 8) for $v = 1, \cdots, N$. At the stationary state, for $\forall v$ in the network, we can get $S^v(\infty) = 0$. These equations can be easily computed numerically by iteration. The final size of the stifler could be obtained as

$$\rho^r = \frac{1}{N}\sum_{v=1}^{N}R^v \quad (10)$$

The system of Eqs. (6, 7 and 8) does not depend on the topological features of the network. Therefore, we could note here that this method could be applied in small world networks, SF networks and ER networks. Indeed, all the topological information enters in the computation of the probability that a node is not effected by its neighbors".

4 Numerical Results

As mentioned above, Monte Carlo (MC) simulation turns out to be accurate in modeling the phase diagram of rumor spreading in complex networks. Therefore, we could check whether our the numerical solutions of Eqs. (6), (7) and (8) is validate or not after comparing with MC simulations. Meanwhile, the MC method costs an expensive memory and CPU time requirement. In our experiments, we also evaluate the RPECA's time complexity compared with MC simulation. The results shows that RPECA could converge much faster than the Monte Carlo method.

Experiment Setup. The network size is 1000 nodes and time is discretized in time-steps. At the beginning of each simulations, a fraction ρ_0 of randomly chosen nodes' states are set as "spreader" and at each time step, a random spreader tries to contact all of its neighbors and influences them following the rules (2,3) mentioned in Part III. The simulation runs until the probability of a node being in spreader state is lower than a threshold value ε. In MC simulations, ε could be seen as the time when the number of spreaders becomes 0.

4.1 Small-World Networks

Two of the most famous small-world networks are the WS small-world network [11] and the NW small-world network [27]. They both originated from an ordered lattice with moderate high connectivity. However, at the following evolution, the previous one is guaranteed by the rule called "randomized re-connecting" and the latter one follows the rule named "randomized edge-plus". In order to avoid the destruction of network connectivity caused by randomized re-connecting, here we apply our method and MC simulations on top of the NW small-world networks. The coinciding between both curves in each sub-figure of Fig. 2 is almost matchless. The results proves that our formula are completely accurate when simulating this "messaging process".

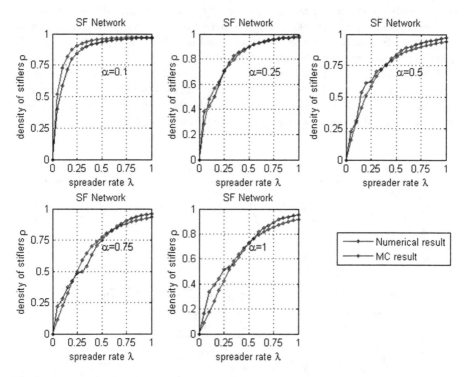

Fig. 2. Average density of stiflers ρ^r, as a function of the spreading rate λ under different stifler rate α for $N = 10^3$. In these set of simulations, we set the probability of "randomized edge-plus" as $p = 0.5$. The red lines represent the result of numerical solutions of our formalism with $\mu = \infty$ (Color figure online).

In addition, with an increasing α value, it is much harder for the system to get a higher consistency rate after one time step. This is because that the higher α is, the easier that a spreader stop sending updating messages. This phenomenon also give us a clue when designing a good eventually consistency strategy that not only increasing the spreading rate λ is important, but also let the spreader keeps trying more times before becoming a stifler. The redundancy mechanism could affect the final performance of eventually consistency in a significant way. In an extremely situation that α value is 1, the eventually consistency could never be satisfied anymore.

Last but not least, it is clearly in Fig. 2 that with a higher λ value, it is much easier for reaching the eventually consistency. This results also suggests that we can apply RPECA to assess in what degree that the consistency is after one time step under certain λ value.

4.2   SF Networks

In Fig. 3, we analyze our formalisms on top of the SF networks composed by 1000 nodes satisfying the power-law distribution $P(k) \sim k^{-\gamma}(\gamma = 3)$. All the results are obtained by averaging over 100 runs with different initial spreaders. It can be seen in Fig. 2 that the deviation between our results and the MC results is less than 0.005, indicating the accuracy and reliability of RPECA.

Figure 3 shows that RPECA not only works on small-world network but also SF (scale-free) network. One interesting phenomenon observed from Fig. 2 shows that in a scale free network, no matter how higher the α is, the eventually consistency could always be reached in one time step as long as we can get an enough high λ. Besides,

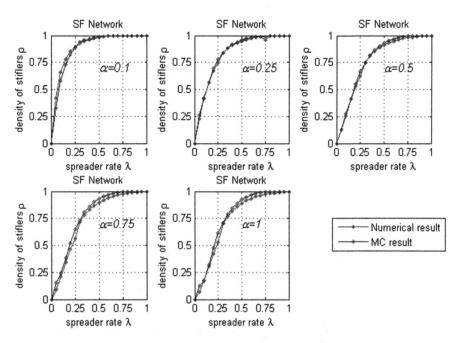

Fig. 3. Average fraction of stifler nodes, ρ^r, as a function of the spreading rate λ for $N = 10^3$, using different values of α. The symbols correspond to MC simulations of the SIR model on top of SF networks with $\gamma = 3$ and the lines represent the numerical solutions of our formulations. Here all neighbors are supposed to be contacted in one time step, so $\mu = \infty$.

compared with small network topology under the same α and λ values, the convergence becomes much easier. Namely, the network topology between replicas could also affect the performance of eventually consistency momentously.

4.3   Time-Complexity in Different Networks

Except understanding the impact of different spreading rate and stifling rate on the rumor evolution process on top of SF and small-world networks, it is of great interest to know the time complexity between numerical solutions and MC simulations.

Figure 4 shows the iteration times t as a function of spreader rate λ under different stifler rate α for $N = 10^3$ at the stationary state on top of SF networks with $\gamma = 3$. Obviously, the numerical simulation takes much less iterations rounds than MC simulation under the same experimental settings. This phenomenon shows that our RPECA could reduce a lot of iteration rounds needed for convergence.

In addition, we also learned that MC simulations takes up more times when decreasing the value of α. That is because the harder that a spreader becomes a stifler, the more time it takes for convergence. We also could observe similar phenomenon in REPCA.

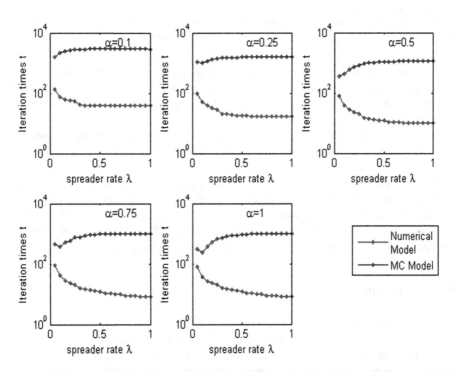

Fig. 4. Iteration times t, as a function of the spreading rate λ, using different stifler rate α. The red line corresponds to numerical simulations for the SIR model on top of SF networks and the blue line represent the MC simulations on the same topology.

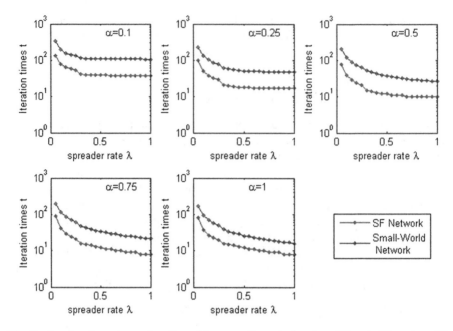

Fig. 5. Iteration times t, as a function of the spreading rate λ, using different stifler rate α. The red line corresponds to numerical simulations for the SIR model on top of SF networks and the blue line represents the same evolution on top of small-world networks.

The last valuable thing we can get from Figs. 2, 3 and 4 is that under certain experiment settings, we could know the approximate degree of consistency among all the replicas, this will give us a good guidance for monitoring the consistency behavior in an cost efficient way.

In Fig. 4 we show that REPCA could converge much faster than MC simulation. Next we compare under the same parameters, how the topology of replica-network could affect the time complexity.

Figure 5 shows the iteration rounds needed for convergence in SF networks and small-world networks. Clearly, compared with the small-world networks, the rumor spreads much faster in SF networks, which is also implicated in Figs. 2 and 3. As we mentioned above, under the same experiment settings, REPCA could get a higher perception of stiflers, which means it is much easier for convergence.

5   Conclusion

As a special case of infirm consistency, eventually consistency has been studied for many years. But little efforts is contributed to how to assess these eventually consistency model. In this work, we first discussed in which aspects are the most popular eventually consistency models in common. Based on the discussion, we found almost all these models are based on "messaging" mechanism. Then we argue that the rumor propagation process is very similar to this messaging mechanism.

After making assumptions on the rumor propagation process, we introduced a general discrete-time markov chain model of rumor spreading on complex networks. By defining a set of discrete-time equations based on markov model, we could compute the probability that a node being in certain kind of states. Our method could be applied in any complex topology and the whole dynamic process is generalized from a contact process (CP) to a reactive process (RP) [13]. We have solved the equations by numerical iterations at the stationary state and got the whole phase diagram of the system. By comparing with the MC simulations, it is proved that our equations are valid, especially in SF networks. We discussed the influence of parameter settings on the degree of consistency. Moreover, it was found that the rumor spreading process performs more efficiently in SF network than small-world network. Also the numerical solution of our model overcomes the high time complexity of MC simulations.

Last but not least, since our model deals with the process by considering each node in the network, it opens the gate of studying the dynamics of rumor spreading in a fine-grained way.

Acknowledgments. This work is supported by The National High Technology Research and Development Program of China (863 Program) No. 2015AA050203; No. 2013AA014800; the Core Electronic Devices, High-end Generic Chips and Basic Software of National Science and Technology Major Projects of China, No. 2013ZX01039002.

References

1. Gilbert, S., Lynch, N.: Brewer's conjecture and the feasibility of consistent, available, partition-tolerant web services. In: ACM SIGACT News, vol. 33, pp. 51–59 (2002)
2. Abadi, D.J.: Consistency tradeoffs in modern distributed database system design: CAP is only part of the story. Computer **2**, 37–42 (2012)
3. Wen, D., Wang, H.-M., Yan, J., Peng, Z.: A rumor-spreading analog on unstructured P2P broadcast mechanism. J. Comput. Res. Dev. **41**, 1460–1465 (2004)
4. Birman, K.: Reliable Distributed Systems Technologies, Web Services and Applications. Springer Science and Business Media, New York (2005)
5. Bailis, P., Venkataraman, S., Franklin, M., Hellerstein, J., Stoica, I.: Probabilistically bounded staleness for practical partial quorums. In: Proceedings of the VLDB Endowment, pp. 776–787 (2012)
6. Zellag, K., Kemme, B.: How consistent is your cloud application? In: Proceedings of the Third ACM Symposium on Cloud Computing (2012)
7. Bermbach, D., Kuhlenkamp, J.: Consistency in distributed storage systems: an overview of models, metrics and measurement approaches. In: Proceedings of the International Conference on Networked Systems (NETYS), vol. 7853, pp.175–189. Springer, Heidelberg (2013)
8. Rahman, M., Golab, W., AuYoung, A., Keeton, K., Wylie, J.: Toward a principled framework for benchmarking consistency. In: Proceedings of the Eighth USENIX Conference on Hot Topics in System Dependability, p. 8. USENIX Association (2012)
9. Golab, W., Li, X., Shah, M.A.: Analyzing consistency properties for fun and profit. In: Proceedings of the 30th Annual ACM SIGACT-SIGOPS Symposium on Principles of Distributed Computing, pp. 197–206. ACM press (2011)

10. Erdos, P., Renyi, A.G.: On the evolution of random graphs. Publ. Math. Inst. Hung. Acad. Sci. **A247**, 529–551 (1955)
11. Watts, D.J., Strongatz, S.H.: Collective dynamics of 'small-world' networks. Nature **393**, 440–442 (1998)
12. Newman, M.E.J., Watts, D.J.: Renormalization group analysis of the small-world network model. Phys. Lett. A **263**, 341–346 (1999)
13. Barabasi, A.L., Albert, R.: Emergence of scalling in random networks. Science **286**, 509–512 (1999)
14. Satorrasr, R.P., Vespignani, A.: Evolution and Structure of the Internet: a Statistical Physics Approach. Cambridge University Press, Cambridge (2004)
15. Caldarelli, G.: ScaSle-Free Networks. Oxford University Press, Oxford (2007)
16. Zanette, D.H.: Dynamics of rumor propagation on small-world networks. Phys. Rev. E. **64**, 041908 (2002)
17. Moreno, Y., Nekovee, M., Pacheco, A.F.: Dynamics of rumor spreading in complex networks. Phys. Rev. E. **69**, 066130 (2004)
18. Dodds, P.S., Watts, D.J.: Universal behavior in a generalized model of contagion. Phys. Rev. Lett. **92**, 218701 (2004)
19. Moreno, Y., Gomez, J.B., Pacheco, A.F.: Epidemic incidence in correlated complex networks. Phys. Rev. E **68**, 035103 (2003)
20. Zanette, D.H.: Critical behavior of propagation on small-world networks. Phys. Rev. E **64**, 050901 (2001)
21. Anderson, R.M., May, R.M.: Infections Disease of Humans. Oxford University Press, Oxford (1991)
22. Gomez, S., Arenas, A.: Discrete-time Markov chain approach to contact-based disease spreading in complex networks. Europhys. Lett. **89**, 38009 (2010)
23. Gomez, S., Arenas, A.: Probabilistic framework for epidemic spreading in complex networks. Int. J. Complex Syst. Sci. **1**, 47–54 (2011)
24. Nekovee, M., Moreno, Y., Bianconi, G., Marsili, M.: Theory of rumor spreading in complex social networks. Physica A **374**, 457–470 (2007)
25. Maki, D.P.: Mathematical Models and Applications, with Emphasis on Social, Life, and Management Sciences. Prentice-Hall, Englewood Cliffs (1973)
26. Daley, D.J., Gani, J.: Epidemic Modelling. Cambridge University Press, Cambridge (2000)
27. Newman, M.E.J., Watts, D.J.: Renormalization group analysis of the small-world network model. Phys. Lett. A **263**, 341–346 (1999)

Efficient Implementation of MIPS Code Generator for the IonMonkey JavaScript Compiler

Tong Ren[1,2(✉)], Shuangbai Xue[2,3], Fei Peng[3], Qing Wang[3], and Xiang Gao[2,3]

[1] University of Chinese Academy of Sciences, Beijing, China
rentong_1979@126.com
[2] Institute of Computing Technology, Chinese Academy of Sciences, Beijing, China
xueshuangbai@ict.ac.cn
[3] Loongson Technologies Corporation Limited, Beijing, China
{pengfei,wangqing,gaoxiang}@loongson.cn

Abstract. Browser is the entry point to cloud computing services, and the performance of JavaScript, with which the web applications are built, has become critically important in the user experience. The key to achieving JavaScript execution efficiency is Just-in-time (JIT) compilation. At present, Firefox is one of the most popular cross platform browsers. However, there is no MIPS code generator in IonMonkey, Firefox's next-generation optimizing JavaScript JIT compiler, leaving the un-performed interpreter the only option to execute Java-Script on MIPS platform in Firefox. In this paper, we managed to implement an efficient and reliable MIPS code generator for IonMonkey. We took an insight into the inner mechanism of IonMonkey, and solved a series of platform-related problems such as double-layer cross platform architecture, patch, jump source chain, and ABI. Additionally, we optimized IonMonkey based on MIPS archi-tecture by using a series of methods such as short-distance jump optimization, range analysis for arithmetic operation, peephole optimization, etc. With the JIT porting and these optimizations, V8 benchmark scores ascended from 38.8 to 957, and the running time of Sunspider benchmark descended from 20428.7 ms to 2689.5 ms. The efficiency of JS engine was significantly improved on MIPS.

Keywords: Javascript · Ionmonkey · Just-In-Time compilation · V8 benchmark · Sunspider benchmark

1 Introduction

Web applications are a critical part of internet infrastructure and are used for banking, email, financial management, online shopping, auctions, social networking, etc. [1]. Almost all the client side of the web applications are developed with JavaScript, and JavaScript is considered as the "assembly language of the Web" [2]. Consequently, the execution efficiency of JavaScript affects web application's user experience seriously.

© Springer International Publishing Switzerland 2015
Y. Chen et al. (Eds.): APPT 2015, LNCS 9231, pp. 73–85, 2015.
DOI: 10.1007/978-3-319-23216-4_6

Given user's hardware device, speed depends on efficiency, and the key to efficiency is Just-in-time (JIT) compilation. But that is not the whole story. Considering the overhead of compilation, it is not wise to compile the function that would only be executed several times. In modern browsers, JavaScript is initially executed with interpreter, slow but doesn't have the compiling overhead. When a function in the JavaScript gets hot–which means the function has been executed many times–the baseline compiler compiles it into native code that could be executed by the machine. The baseline compilation is accompanied by few optimization and small overhead. When the function gets hotter, the advanced compiler recompiles it with more optimizations, leading to more overhead. As the hot spot gets executed more times in the efficient way, the compiling overhead would be diluted.

MIPS (originally an acronym for Microprocessor without Interlocked Pipeline Stages) is a reduced instruction set computer (RISC) instruction set (ISA) developed by MIPS Technologies [3]. Although MIPS Technologies was acquired by Imagination Technologies in 2012, MIPS ISA doesn't disappear from market. The research and develop team of MIPS Technologies survives, and continues to launch new MIPS processors. Besides, companies like Loongson Technology have licensed the MIPS ISA and designed processors independently. In fact, MIPS implementations are still popular and widely used.

Firefox is one of the most popular browsers. Unlike Microsoft's closed source and Windows-only Internet Explorer, Firefox is open source and cross platform, making the web applications and cloud computing services available on platforms other than x86 and Windows. However, there is no MIPS code generator in IonMonkey, Firefox's next-generation optimizing JavaScript JIT compiler, leaving the un-performed interpreter the only option. Figure 1 shows the principle and situation of JS engine in Firefox.

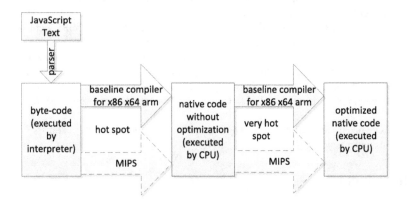

Fig. 1. JS engine in Firefox

Poor performance of the interpreter based JS engine impedes the usability of web services on MIPS platform, and Firefox is kept away from the potential market. We implement the MIPS code generator for IonMonkey, bridging the gap between MIPS and Firefox.

We identify our technical contributions as:

- A complete and efficient implementation of MIPS code generator for baseline compiler and IonMonkey.
- Innovatively introducing the double-layer cross-platform design, to reconcile the contradiction between reliability and efficiency.
- Applying a series of platform related optimizations, to eliminate the inefficiencies that come with the cross-platform MacroAssembler.

2 Related Work

2.1 Nitro's MacroAssembler

In Nitro, the JIT compiler of Apple's WebKit JavaScript Engine, platform independence is achieved by its MacroAssembler, an elegantly-designed component that can be used to emit machine code for multiple target architectures: all of x86, x86-64, ARM and MIPS assembly are supported through the same C++ interface. This abstraction is the reason that only one implementation of the compiler is needed for all architectures, which has been a clear win in terms of cross-platform feature additions and maintainability [4]. The Nitro's MacroAssembler is also reused in JaegerMonkey, the JIT compiler of Firefox's previous JavaScript Engine. Figure 2 shows the JaegerMonkey's machine-code-emitting component imported from Nitro.

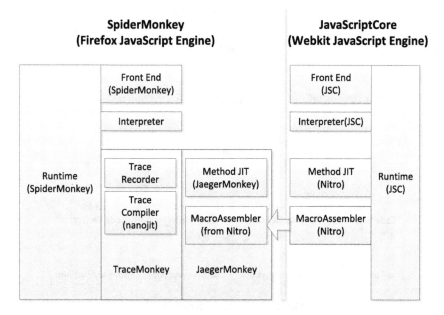

Fig. 2. Assembler from Apple

However, MacroAssembler forces all other architectures to behave in the x86 way. For example, the MacroAssembler has a two-address interface instead of a three-address interface. This means that instead of having methods like add(dest, op1, op2), it has methods like add (op1, op2), where the operation implicitly stores its result in its first operand. Though it does correspond to the x86 instruction set, this sort of interface is not great for systems where there are more registers (like on MIPS), and forces the compiler to shuffle registers around a lot [5]. The bias towards x86 badly undermines the efficiency of other platforms.

2.2   Hierarchy of IonMonkey

In IonMonkey, intermediate representation (IR) is introduced to shield the diversity of architecture for upper layer modules of the compiler. There are three kind of IR: bytecode, Middle-level IR (MIR) and Low-level IR (LIR). LIR is generated from MIR, MIR is generated from bytecode, and bytecode is generated from JavaScript text. These IRs are for different purpose. Bytecode could be executed by the interpreter. MIR is for platform independent optimization, such as loop-invariant code motion, global value numbering, dead code elimination, etc. [6]. LIR focuses on code generation. When the code generator is fed with LIR instructions, it produces native code that could be executed by the processor. LIR is augmented on a per-platform basis. There are shared LIR instructions that are expected to work on every platform, but platforms can also introduce their own LIR only available for a certain CPU [7]. There have been Code Generators for x86, x64 and arm, while MIPS's is in absence (Fig. 3).

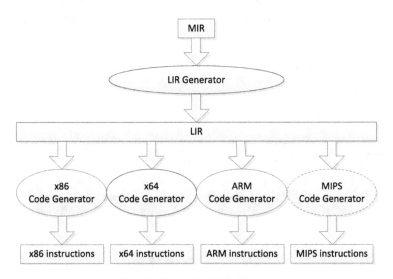

Fig. 3. Hierarchy of IonMonkey

3 Porting

3.1 Double-Layer Cross Platform

Reliability always comes first, and the best way to ensure reliability is to reuse existing robust code. As is shown in Fig. 4, the x86 Code Generator is based on Nitro's x86 Assembler, while Nitro's MIPS MacroAssembler has an x86-style interface–replacing Nitro's x86 Assembler with Nitro's MIPS MacroAssembler, then we get the MIPS Code Generator. The thing left is to deal with the incompatible parts not covered by Nitro's platform independent MacroAssembler interface.

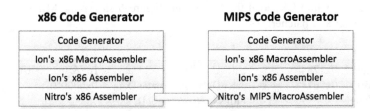

Fig. 4. Hierarchy of Ion's Code Generator

We call the Hierarchy of our IonMonkey as "double-layer cross platform", since Nitro's MacroAssembler is another platform independent layer beneath the cross platform LIR interface.

3.2 Patch

During the process of code generation, there exist moments that the constant to embed into the current instruction, such as the supposed object type in the polymorphic inline cache (PIC) [8], is not known yet. The location of the constant in the instruction stream is recorded, and the constant would be written into that location when its value is determined. With the location information, the constant could also be modified on-the-fly. For example, the supposed object type could be modified to make a more likely guess. The location of the constant is called a patch, and the instruction contain the constant is an "instruction with patch". Modifying the constant is called "patch write".

In Ion's x86 Assembler, there are instructions as cmplWithPatch, pushWithPatch, etc., and all the patchable parts are the last four bytes of the instructions. The address of next instruction is recorded as handle of the patch, and the patcher would write the constant into the four bytes before that address. Figure 5 shows the x86 implementation of patch and patcher:

cmpl 0x12345678, %eax label: (a) cmplWithPatch	*((int *)(label-4)) = patchData; (b) patch write

Fig. 5. x86 implementation of patch and patcher

However, the assertion about the last four bytes thing doesn't keep true for fixed length instruction set as MIPS. Every MIPS instruction only occupies four bytes, and 6 bits of the four bytes act as operation code. As a result, there is no way to fill four bytes data into a single MIPS instruction. Two instructions are needed, and the classic MIPS combination is LUI and ORI: LUI load 16 bits immediate data into the upper half of the 32 bit register, while ORI load the lower half. Figure 6 shows the MIPS implementation of patch and patcher:

label: lui r1, 0x1234
    ori r1, 0x5678
    cmpl
 	
(a) cmplWithPatch
	patchDataHi = (patchData >> 16) & 0x0000ffff;
	patchDataLow = patchData & 0x0000ffff;
	luiIns = *((int *)label);
	oriIns = *((int *)(label+4));
	luiIns = luiIns & 0xffff0000;
	luiIns = luiIns | patchDataHi
	oriIns = oriIns & 0xffff0000;
	oriIns = oriIns | patchDataLow
	(b) patch write

Fig. 6. MIPS implementation of patch and patcher

3.3   Jump Source Chain

A location in the instruction stream is represented as a label object in the compiler which maintain a pointer targeting on that location. To bind the label means to confirm the exact position of the label and record it in the label object.

Before the label is bound, the label object leading a list of jump instructions targeting on this label, and all jump instructions targeting on this label would be added into the list. We call the list as jump source chain.

By the time the label gets bound, all the jump instructions in the list get linked to the bound location.

After the binding, all later jump instructions targeting on this label would be linked to the bound location recorded in the label object.

On x86 platform, the list node of the jump source chain is inlined in the jump instruction: since the list node only need to exist before the label is bound, the last four bytes of the jump instruction which are reserved for the target address that has not been determined could act as the list node temporally. When the label got bound, the list node is of no use, and the target address could take place of it.

On MIPS, we use the place of NOP instruction in the delay-slot of the jump instruction to inline the list node. When the jump instruction got bound, the NOP instruction should be recovered.

3.4 ABI

When calling C++ function from JS code, layout of the stack and parameters should obey the Application Binary Interface (ABI), which is platform-dependent. We implemented the MIPS O32 ABI specified in [16].

3.5 Truncate

In the case of TRUNCATE instruction, When the source value is Infinity, NaN, or rounds to an integer outside the range -2^{31} to $2^{31}-1$, the result cannot be represented correctly by an integer, and an invalid value would be generated and checked. The invalid value is 0x80000000 on x86, and it's 0x7fffffff on MIPS.

4 Optimization

Although the double-layer cross-platform design simplified our implementation of the MIPS Code Generator, it also introduced inefficiencies since the Nitro's MacroAssembler forces MIPS to act in the x86 way. More MIPS instructions than necessary are emitted and executed.

The key concept of code generator optimization is that the less instruction emitted the better. We manually traverse the implementation of the code generator and try to eliminate as much unnecessary instructions as possible. A series of optimization methods are applied to the code generator: Replacing jump instruction template with short-distance jump decreases the number of instructions emitted; Range analysis attempts to avoid unnecessary overflow check; Peephole optimization takes advantage of local information and tries to eliminate redundant instructions; Special treatment for frequent tasks as regular expression parsing also promote the overall performance.

4.1 Short-Distance Jump

In Nitro's MacroAssembler, internal jump is implemented as a template consists of 6 MIPS instructions. As is shown in List 1, the template is designed to be able to jump to any target within the 4 GB address space (Fig. 7).

beq r1, r2, relativeToTarget	bne r1, r2, label	bne r1, r2, label
nop	nop	nop
beq r0, r0, label	j target	lui tmpReg, targetUpper16bits
nop	nop	ori tmpReg, targetLower16bits
nop	nop	jr tmpReg
nop	nop	nop
label:	label:	label:
(a) Form 1	(b) Form 2	(c) Form 3

Fig. 7. Template for jump in Nitro's MacroAssembler

The template has 3 forms: Form 1 for short-distance jump within 32767 instructions before or after the first instruction of the template; Form 2 for middle-distance jump within the same 256 MB aligned segment the 4th instruction of the template lies; Form 3 for long-distance jump. In form 1, the relative address is encoded in the instructions, and the addresses of the jump source and destination have no effect on the behavior of the template. But in form 2, if the 256 MB condition was break, the template would jump to wrong place. When this happened, the template should turn to form 3. Even form 3 is not free from problems: if the address of the target was changed, the instructions contain the address should get updated.

During the process of code generation, the MacroAssembler doesn't know how many instructions would be emitted, so it maintains a dynamic buffer to hold the emitted instructions. When the buffer is full, the MacroAssembler would reallocate a new buffer twice the size of the old buffer, and copy all the instructions into the new buffer. This causes the source address and target address of the internal jump changed, and it is possible that the 6 instructions targeting on wrong address. To handle this situation, the MacroAssembler records all the internal jumps, and fixes them every time the buffer gets copied.

The fixing after each buffer copy surely is unnecessary. It's better to fill internal jump templates after the last copy.

Furthermore, there are chances to cut form 1 of the template into 2 instructions in the code generator. Obviously, the last four instructions does nothing and are equal to nops. The reason they are there is that when the template emitted, the target address is not known, so the place in the buffer should be retained in case the jump distance is not so short. Luckily, in the code generator, it is not rare that we do know the distance between the jump source and the destination which is also very short. In these cases, we emit the MIPS short-distance jump instruction instead of the fat template.

When emitting jump template with bound label, we could also calculate the distance and determine whether the short-distance jump instruction is applicable.

This method here brings triple goods: the number of instructions the processor needs to execute decreases which means increasing in efficiency, the size of the generated code minifies which is good for the cache with limited capacity, and the fixing operation after each buffer copy is eliminated.

4.2   Range Analysis

In the JavaScript specification, a number can be either a 32-bit signed integer or 64-bit IEEE 754 floating-point; JavaScript does not explicitly distinguish between them [12, 13]. Since the common case is that numeric values are integers and because floating point operations are more expensive, all major JavaScript implementations attempt to represent numbers as integers when possible [9]. Considering correctness, overflow checks are inserted after integer arithmetic operations.

mul imm32(rhs), lhs	mul imm32(rhs), lhs
overflow check	if(canOverFlow())
	overflow check
(a)without range analysis	(b)with range analysis

Fig. 8. Range analysis optimization

We applied range analysis method to eliminate provably unnecessary overflow checks. Figure 8 shows the pseudo-code before and after the optimization.

4.3 Peephole Optimization

The idea of peephole optimization is to take advantage of local information to eliminate redundant instructions. In this paper, we mainly applied this method to the test-and-conditional jump and compare-and-conditional jump instruction sequence.

In 86 processors, every arithmetic operation including bitwise logical instructions modifies flags such as the carry flag, the sign flag, the overflow flag and the zero flag according to the value of the result. The state of these flags decides the behavior of subsequent conditional jump instructions. However, these flags don't exist in the MIPS architecture. The MIPS style is to calculate the flag by software before using it.

In order to implement the x86 style conditional jump, Nitro's MacroAssembler reserves two temp registers from the register allocator to hold back the data involved in the last arithmetic operation. The data in these two registers would be used to generate flags desired by following conditional jump instructions. In another word, instead of holding back the flags by hardware, the MacroAssembler holds back the data to generate the flags.

It is a giant pain to push operands into these two temp registers for all the arithmetic operations. Fortunately, we don't have to do this. In Ion's code generator, all the flags used by conditional jumps are generated by two instructions: test and compare. The test instruction performs a bitwise AND on two operands, and the compare instruction performs subtraction on two operands. Neither of the two instructions save the computing result, they only modify the flags.

In the test-and-conditional jump or compare-and-conditional jump sequences, there are many chances to eliminate redundant instructions. For example, test instruction with identical operands could be optimized as is shown in Fig. 9:

mov op1, cmpTemp1	mov op1, cmpTemp2
mov op1, cmpTemp2	mov zero, cmpTemp1
and cmpTemp2, cmpTemp1	
mov zero, cmpTemp1	
(a) before optimization	(b) after optimization

Fig. 9. Optimization for test(op1, op1)

Another example, compare two registers and conditional jump could be optimized as is shown in Fig. 10:

mov r1, cmpTemp1	beq r1, r2, target
mov r2, cmpTemp2	nop
beq cmpTemp1, cmpTemp2, target	
nop	
(a) before optimization	(b) after optimization

Fig. 10. Optimization for compare two registers and conditional jump

There are much more redundant instructions in the code generator that could be eliminated by means of peephole optimization. The ultimate goal is to turn the code generator into a totally MIPS style.

4.4 Compiler Parameter Tuning

Regular expressions are widely used in JS based applications, and the speed of parsing regular expressions has a considerable impact on the overall performance of JS engine. Therefor, JS engine usually integrates an extra regular expression engine to accelerate the regular expression parsing tasks.

Yarr is a splendid regular expression engine that's part of JavaScriptCore, the Apple's JS engine. It is also reused in Google's Chromium and Mozilla's Firefox. But yarr is not enabled by default in Firefox, we need to turn on the switch by adding the compiler parameter explicitly.

Besides, other compiler parameters used in compiling the JS engine also matters. These parameters determine how the JS engine itself is compiled, and affect the execution efficiency of the JS engine, which dominates the overhead of the JIT compiling. We tuned the parameters and got measurable increase in the overall performance.

5   Evaluation

To evaluate our work, we tested for correctness with Mozilla's large repository of regression tests, and measured the impact of our optimization with the commonly available benchmark suites [9]. Table 1 shows the details of our testing environment.

Table 1. Testing environment

CPU	Loongson3A (MIPS compatible processor)
Memory	4 GB
OS	Fedora 13
OS kernel	Linux 2.6.36.3+
GCC	GCC 4.4.4 (Red Hat 4.4.4-14)
Firefox	Version 24 ESR

5.1 Correctness

Table 2. Mozilla's regression test set

SUM	Success	TimeOut	Asm	Ion	BaseLine	Basic
3687	3667	0	19	0	0	1

Mozilla's regression test set consists of 3687 test cases. As is shown in Table 2, we passed 3667 and failed 20. We didn't implement Asm, which is another compiler in Firefox, and that is why we didn't pass the test cases in this category. "bug839215.js" in the Basic category failed in allocating large amount of memory, and it has been removed from the test set in the latest version of Firefox. To sum up, we can safely say that we have passed all the regression tests. Furthermore, there is no halting or error occurred in the later performance tests and daily use.

5.2 Performance

There are two benchmark suites which are generally used to measure JavaScript JIT compilers: the v8bench suite developed by Google [10] and the Sunspider benchmark suite developed by Apple [11]. The v8bench runs representative test cases and synthesizes a score as evaluation of the JS engine, the higher the better. The SunSpider measures the time consumed to finish the test, the less the better.

We ran the benchmark suites after each addition of our optimizations. The results are summarized in Figs. 11 and 12. For convenience, we call the interpreter-only JS engine as Algorithm 1, JS engine with IonMonkey is Algorithm 2, after the short-distance jump optimization and range analysis is Algorithm 3, with the peephole optimization, it's Algorithm 4, and finally, all the optimizations above with the compiler parameter tuning is Algorithm 5.

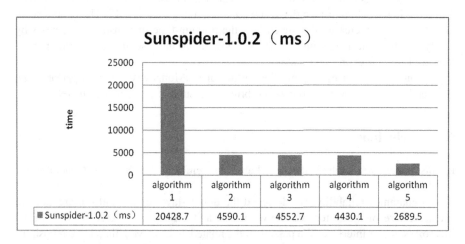

Fig. 11. Sunspider benchmark results, less time is better

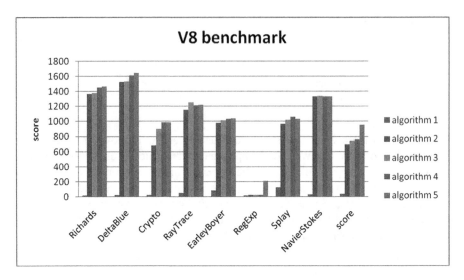

Fig. 12. V8 benchmark results, higher score is better

Comparing Algorithm 2 to Algorithm 1, we can see that the performance increases tremendously. As is shown in Fig. 12, the Spark of JIT transforms the dwarfish car into a towering rocket.

Algorithm 3 results in outstanding performance promotion in Crypto and RayTrace. Obviously, Range analysis technique is the secret sauce for these intense numeric computing tasks.

Algorithm 4 gets small but measurable overall performance increase. It means that the proportion of the optimized part is low. If we look around and apply peephole optimization to more part of the code generator, we would gain more. In fact, the code generator is shared from x86, and the implementation is far from perfect for MIPS.

Algorithm 5 is a special treatment for regular expression, and its effect is evident. The score in the subtask of RegExp increases from the ground to 210. The overall score of v8bench also increased this much, and the running time of Sunspider decreases by nearly a half. From the result, we can see how much the test suites value the performance of regular expression parsing.

To summarize our evaluation, the porting of IonMonkey results in a performance leap, and every following optimization brings measurable performance increase.

6   Conclusions

In this paper, we implemented a reliable and efficient MIPS Code Generator for IonMonkey.

To guarantee reliability, we designed the double-layer cross platform architecture and took care of the differences between x86 and MIPS not covered by the Nitro's MacroAssembler interface. We passed all the related cases in Mozilla's large repository of regression tests, which is a strong prove of correctness. In comparison with the inefficient interpreter, the porting of IonMonkey results in a performance leap.

Additionally, we applied a series of platform-related optimizations, such as short-distance jump, range analysis for arithmetic operation, peephole optimization, etc. Each of these optimizations brings measurable performance increase.

Combing the double-layer cross platform design and the following optimizations, we reconciled the contradiction between reliability and performance.

References

1. Rewatkar, L.R., Lanjewar, U.L.: Implementation of cloud computing on web application. In: International Journal of Computer Applications, pp. 28–32 (2010)
2. Hanselman, S.: JavaScript is Assembly Language for the Web: Part 2 - Madness or just Insanity (2011). http://www.hanselman.com/blog/JavaScriptIsAssemblyLanguageForTheWebPart2 MadnessOrJustInsanity.aspx
3. MIPS instruction set. http://en.wikipedia.org/wiki/MIPS_instruction_set
4. Chris, L.: Picky monkeys PIC ARM (2011). http://blog.cdleary.com/2011/02/picky-monkeys-pic-arm/
5. Andy, W.: JavaScriptCore, the WebKit JS implementation (2011). https://wingolog.org/archives/2011/10/28/javascriptcore-the-webkit-js-implementation
6. MIR. https://wiki.mozilla.org/IonMonkey/MIR
7. LIR. https://wiki.mozilla.org/IonMonkey/LIR
8. Chris L.: PICing on Javascript for fun and profit (2010). http://blog.cdleary.com/2010/09/picing-on-javascript-for-fun-and-profit/
9. Pearl, R., Sullivan, M.: Range Analysis for the IonMonkey JavaScript Compiler (2012). http://www.endofunctor.org/∼cmplrz/paper.pdf
10. Google v8bench javascript benchmark. https://v8.googlecode.com/svn/data/benchmarks/current/revisions.html
11. WebKit.: Sunspider javascript benchmark. http://www.webkit.org/perf/sunspider/sunspider.html
12. JavaScript Language Specification v1.1 (1996). http://www.planetpdf.com/codecuts/pdfs/tutorial/jsspec.pdf
13. IEEE Computer Society. IEEE Standard for Floating-Point Arithmetic (2008)
14. Intel x86 Instruction Set. http://www.intel.com/content/dam/www/public/us/en/documents/manuals/64-ia-32-architectures-software-developer-instruction-set-reference-manual-325383.pdf
15. MIPS Instruction Set. http://www.cs.cmu.edu/afs/cs/academic/class/15740-f97/public/doc/mips-isa.pdf
16. MIPS O32 ABI. http://math-atlas.sourceforge.net/devel/assembly/mipsabi32.pdf

Effects of Quenched Disorder on Liquid Crystal: A Simulation of Rough Cylinder Confinement

Qing Ji[(✉)]

Chief Scientist of HPC Application, HPC Division,
State Key Laboratory of High-End Server and Storage Technology,
Inspur Group, Jinan, Shangdong, People's Republic of China
jiqing@inspur.com

Abstract. Quenched disorder (QD) and surface field are two key factors in nano-confinement researches. Despite decades of development, distinguishing the two factors is still challenging. To explore this issue, liquid crystals (LCs) confined in both smooth and rough cylinders are simulated and compared with the bulk LCs. The rough cylinders are aperiodical and produced firstly via randomly spherical indentation. Results show that QD reduces the order of orientation and translation, lessens the anisotropy of diffusion and shortens the rotational correlation time of the confined LCs with respect to the surface field. The intensity of the QD effects depends on the magnitude of the roughness of cylinders. In addition, the anisotropic diffusion of LCs exhibits a circular pattern when LCs system are cooled from the isotropic phase to the smectic phase. The simulated anisotropic diffusion validates the affine transformation model for the Bulk system in the isotropic and nematic phases. The model, however, underestimates the anisotropy of the confined systems. These results are helpful to develop physical models and explain experimental phenomena for confinement researches.

Keywords: Liquid crystal · Confinement · Disorder · Roughness · KKLZ and affine transformation model

1 Introduction

Nano-confinement is a common phenomenon in the natural world and our daily life [1, 2]. The confinement introduces several different factors: the surface field, the quenched disorder (QD), the low dimensionality (slit confinement is two-dimensional and cylinder confinement is one-dimensional), and so on [3, 4]. The surface field originates from the finite size and the QD derives from the surface roughness.

Liquid crystals (LCs) are popular probes for the research of confinement [2]. Generally LCs exhibit a variety of phases as a function of temperature, concentration and composition of solutions. The phases include isotropic (I), nematic (N), smectic (S) and crystal (C) phases, etc. In each phase, LCs show certain ordered structure and activated mobility. The former are characterized by the orientational order and translational order; the latter by the diffusion and rotation, respectively.

© Springer International Publishing Switzerland 2015
Y. Chen et al. (Eds.): APPT 2015, LNCS 9231, pp. 86–102, 2015.
DOI: 10.1007/978-3-319-23216-4_7

In experiments, LCs have been capillarily impregnated into a mesoporous solid such as aerogels, aerosil nano-particles and vycor glass [5–10]. It has been found that the orientational order of the confined LCs is larger than that of the bulk LCs at high temperature (called the para-nematic phase) [11–13]. The I-N and N-S phase transitions have been also observed to delay or be weakened [11, 14–20]. However, distinguishing the effect of surface field and QD via experiments alone is obfuscated by challenges with both the instruments' resolution at the relevant length- and timescales and the difficulties of quantitatively controlling the roughness of the samples' surface [3, 21–24].

In simulation, from the early Lebwohl–Lasher model to the late Gay-Berne (GB) model, the basic physical model for the pure Bulk LCs has been built [5, 25–27]. The GB model is very popular in confinement studies, most of which are smooth and especially for the slit confinement [27–33]. In contrast, the simulations of the confined LCs with the quenched disorder are limited. Cheung contributed on this issue for the isotropic and nematic phases [34, 35]. In his study, the surface roughness was introduced by embedding a few molecules with random positions and orientations on the wall surface. In the embedding method, the surface roughness exactly depends on the molecular size. That is to say, the magnitude of the roughness is relatively small.

In fact, modeling rough walls is not a new problem. Previous articles showed that there were at least four other kinds of the methods available. First, building the walls with sinusoidal function has been suggested by Jabbarzadeh [36]. Second, Pellenq has prepared a rough pore comprised of several strips, which have the same thickness but different random diameters [37]. Third, Kuchta randomly set the interaction parameters between the wall and the particles inside: attractive, neutral and repulsive with respect to the smooth pore model [38, 39]. Last, Strickland generated a porous material by liquid–liquid phase separation in which once the desired pore size was reached, one phase was frozen, while the other was split into a binary mixture [40]. It is a pity that all the methods above are not helpful enough in terms of the features of experimental container [11, 41, 42]. The experimental containers are continuous cylinders and have significant roughness on the nanometer scale. Therefore, in the first two methods (sinusoid and strips), their rough walls cannot avoid periodicity. The third method (letting the walls possess different interactions) is apparently different from the real experimental case. Using phase separation to produce a rough wall is a good method. However, it is very easy to lose the connectivity during the phase separation. Thus we have to use another method to produce a rough wall which matches the feature of the experiments.

This paper first introduced the spherical indentation to construct the rough walls. Three rough cylinders (RW1, RW2 and RW3) were constructed with different shapes and magnitude of roughness. Via comparison of the characteristics of LCs in the three RWs with those in the smooth cylinder and the bulk, the effects of the surface field and the quenched disorder can be distinguished relatively clearly. The typical structural ordering and dynamical properties of LCs in the isotropic, nematic and smectic phase were addressed.

2 Models and Simulation Details

In this study, all quantities are expressed in conventional reduced units, with σ_0 and ε_0 being the units of length and energy, respectively. Thus, the temperature is given in units of ε_0/k_B, the pressure is in units of ε_0/σ_0^3, the momentum of inertia is in units of $m\sigma_0^2$ and the number density is in units of $1/\sigma_0^3$. Here k_B is the Boltzmann constant.

2.1 Description of Models

Five systems were simulated: the Bulk, the smooth wall (radius $r = 10$, S10) and the three rough cylinders (radius $r \sim 10$, RW1, RW2 and RW3). The radii of 10 represented about 1/4 size of the real experiment dimension (16 nm), if the short diameter of

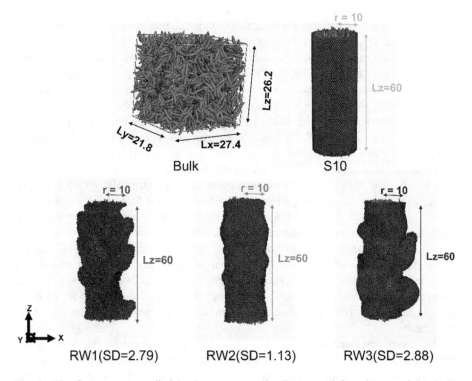

Fig. 1. The five systems studied in the present study. From top left to bottom right: Bulk; Smooth cylinder (S10); Rough cylinder 1 (RW1); Rough cylinder 2 (RW2) and Rough cylinder 3 (RW3). The green ellipses are liquid crystals in Gay–Berne model (4.4, 20, 1, 1) and the blue spheres are walls with Lennard-Jones 12-6 potential. The cell dimensions of each system are shown in reduced unit. The densities of all LCs are 0.153 [43]. All cylinders are set along the Z-axis. The standard deviation (SD) of the radius in the XY-plane of each rough cylinder is shown. It is a measure of the roughness. Thus, the relative roughness of the three rough cylinders is RW1 $\approx$ RW3 > RW2. The same color will be used for the following figures. They are: black for Bulk, red for RW1, green for RW2, blue for RW3 and light blue for S10 (Color figure online).

a simulated LC particle could be compared to that of 4-n-octyl-4-cyanobiphenyl 4 Å [42]. A sketch of the five systems is shown in Fig. 1, which includes the cell dimensions for each system. Periodic boundary conditions were applied in the three dimensions for the Bulk system and along the cylinder channel (Z-axis) for the confined systems, which are S10, RW1, RW2 and RW3.

The interactions between LC particles were expressed by the pair potential proposed by Gay and Berne (GB) for axially symmetric particles [44]. The GB potential is parameterized by four variables κ, κ', v and μ. The Greek term κ denotes the length-to-breadth ratio of the molecule, while κ' denotes the ratio of the potential well depths between the side-by-side and the end-to-end configurations. The exponent v and μ are adjustable parameters that have been introduced to tune the shape of the anisotropic interaction, by affecting the nematic and smectic ordering ability of the particles in a subtle way. The four parameters were (4.4, 20, 1, 1) in the present study as in many previous papers [26, 43, 45–47]. Compared with other parameter settings, the setting provided more stable nematic and smectic A phases, which are closer to the experiment [25, 26]. The potential of the wall was chosen as Lennard-Jones 12-6 (LJ) interaction. The interactions between the LJ and GB were set same as that between GBs except for the symmetries. The LJ particle had three-axes $a = b = c = 1$ and the GB particle had $a = b = c/4.4$. More descriptions of the two models have been shown in previous works [43, 48, 49].

2.2   Model Construction

The Bulk system consisted of 2400 LC particles with cell dimension Lx = 27.4, Ly = 21.8 and Lz = 26.2. The density of the system was $\rho = 0.153$ which was the equilibrium density of the bulk liquid crystal at pressure P = 2.0 and temperature T = 1.9 [43]. Using this initial configuration, the system was cooled down from T = 1.9 to T = 0.8 with increment of 0.05. At each temperature, we ran 60,000 canonical ensemble (NVT) simulation cycles for equilibration and 60,000 cycles for data collection and averaging. The cooling simulation was applied to all the other systems. The equilibration of the simulation was confirmed by the evolution of the potential energy and temperature. The constant pressure (NPT) ensemble was only used for the Bulk system with pressure P = 2.0 in a heating process from T = 0.8 to T = 1.9 from a crystalline initial configuration as in the previous study [47].

The S10 system comprised N = 2885 particles. The cylinder wall of S10 had the pore length Lz = 60 and the radius $r = 10$ as shown in Fig. 1. Isotropic initial configurations of S10 were obtained after the full melting and thermalization of initial crystalline arrangements, obtained after 300,000 steps of NVT simulation at temperature T = 1.9. With the initial configuration, the same cooling simulation was conducted as that for the Bulk system.

The rough cylinders RW1, RW2 and RW3 experienced the same conduction as the S10 did except for the introduction of roughness. The roughness was created via indenting random locations on the surface of the S10 with a spherical indenter. The indenter repels all atoms that touch it and then deforms the smooth wall to a rough wall.

The idea was similar to that of a boxer punching a sandbag. Mathematically, the force exerted by a spherical indenter of radius R is given by:

$$F(r) = -k \times (l - R)^2 \tag{1}$$

where k was the specified force constant and l was the distance from the center of the indenter. Thus, $l < R$ meant the spherical indenter had an action on the wall and $l > R$ meant the wall was out of the reach of the indenter. The force was repulsive and F (r) = 0 for $l \geq R$. k was set to 1000 in the calculation. The function was applied via the command "fix indent" in open source simulation engine LAMMPS (2008) [50].

There were three types of random values in the setting of the indentation. First, the radius R began at a random value between 1 and 10 and shrank to a random smaller value. Second, the centers of the indenters were located at random coordinates (x and y randomly distribute between −15 and 15 and z distributes from −25 to 25). Third, the velocities of the indenter were distributed randomly between −30 and 30 in x and y direction and between 20 and 30 in z direction. This design of the indentation approximately reproduced the process of the experiment in which a crystalline silicon substrate was electrochemically anodized in a hydrogen fluoride (HF) electrolyte solution [11, 41, 42]. One needed to delete the overlapped wall particles if they exist at the final structure. More details about the command setting can be found in the manual of LAMMPS (2008) [50].

Table 1. The disorder information of the three rough cylinders. The radii in transverse section (XY plane) of each cylinder wall were listed by the average, maximum and minimum values. Standard deviation of the radii was a measure of roughness and listed in the last column.

Model	Average radius	Maximum radius	Minimum radius	Standard deviation
RW1	10.73	17.97	1.21	2.79
RW2	9.94	13.42	5.13	1.13
RW3	10.78	19.56	1.03	2.88

Via the indentation method, three rough cylinders RW1, RW2 and RW3 were produced. The average, maximum and minimum radii of the three cylinders in the transverse section (parallel to XY-plane) were listed in Table 1. The average radii were 10.73, 9.94 and 10.78 for RW1, RW2 and RW3 correspondingly. The standard deviation (SD) was a measure of roughness in this study. The SD for RW1, RW2 and RW3 are 2.79, 1.23 and 2.88 respectively. This implied that the relative magnitude of the roughness was RW1 ≈ 2*RW2 ≈ RW3. The structure of the RW2 wall was extracted from the trajectory which was used to construct RW1. Thus, the comparison between RW1 and RW2 characterized the difference of roughness magnitude and the comparison between RW1 and RW3 characterized the difference of roughness shape.

2.3   Simulation Details

We conducted molecular dynamics (MD) simulation via the LAMMPS (2008) software package, developed by Sandia National Laboratories, in the canonical NVT ensemble [50]. The Nose-Hoover temperature thermostat was applied and the integration time step was set to 0.002. The intermolecular interactions were truncated at $r_c = 5.5 \ \sigma_0$ and no long-range corrections were applied as the previous study [43].

Please notice that the NVT ensemble might not appear as the most suitable ensemble to investigate the phase transition. For instance, it missed the observation of true first order transitions along constant density paths [43]. The ensemble was used in the present study for three reasons. First, the box shape fluctuations are almost impossible in the situation of rigid confinement, which is the interest of the studies [43, 48, 49]. Second, the LAMMPS does not provide the pressure control for a system with fixed atoms. Third, the drawback of NVT ensemble did not significantly change the resolution of the quenched disorder study. The major character of the confinement has been found in the ensemble [43].

3   Results and Discussion

The differences between the effect of quenched disorder and surface field were explored in terms of structure and dynamics respectively. The former comprised the orientational order and the translation order, and the latter included the diffusion and the rotation as reported below.

3.1   Orientational Order

The orientational order characterizes the tendency of the LC particles to align along the director. The order is a measure of the phase transition between the isotropic phase and the nematic phase (I-N). The parameter of the order S was calculated as:

$$S = \ <0.5 \times [3 * (\hat{u}_i \bullet \hat{u}_e)^2 - 1] > \tag{2}$$

where, $\hat{u}_i \bullet \hat{u}_e$ was the dot product between the principal axis of the particle i and that of the corresponding eigenvector e, which maximized S. The parameter ranged from -0.5 to 1; -0.5 indicated perfectly a perpendicular oriented system; 0 indicated a fully orientationally disordered fluid and 1 indicated a perfectly parallel oriented system (Fig. 2).

A Landau–de Gennes model for the confined LC system has been developed by Kutnjak, Kralj, Lahajnar and Zumer (KKLZ model) and applied to analyze experimental data [11, 16, 51]. In this model, the free energy f was described as:

$$f = tq^2 - 2q^3 + q^4 - q\sigma + kq^2 \tag{3}$$

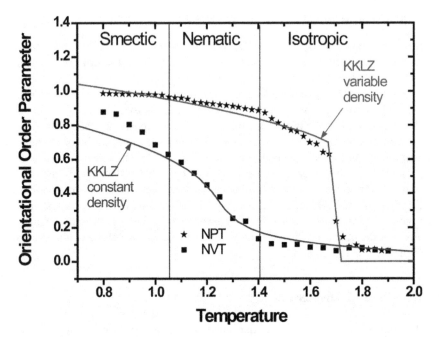

Fig. 2. The orientational order parameter as a function of temperature. The star and square labels are the data of constant pressure (NPT, variable density) and constant volume (NVT, constant density) simulation respectively. The red and blue lines were calculated from a Landau-de Gennes model (KKLZ model) and fittings for the NPT and NVT data respectively [16, 51]. The parameters of the NPT fitting were: the effect of quenched disorder $\kappa = 0$ and the effective surface field $\sigma = 0$. Those parameter of the NVT fitting were $\kappa = 1.1$ and $\sigma = 0.7$. Both fittings were calibrated by the temperature and the orientational order parameter at $T = 1.7$ [11]. The two fitting of the KKLZ models agreed with the simulation data in the nematic and isotropic phase. The boundaries of different phases were for the NVT Bulk system. From right to left: isotropic, nematic and smectic phases. They were abbreviated as I, N and S respectively in the following.

where q was the scaled orientational order parameter $q = S/S_{I-N}$, t was the reduced temperature; σ was the effective surface field and k was the quenched disordering. Minimalization of f yields the equilibrium q.

The KKLZ model was applied to the present simulation data as shown in Fig. 3. The simulation data of the bulk systems were in two ensembles: constant volume (NVT) and constant pressure (NPT) in which densities were constant and variable, respectively. As shown in the figure, the prediction of the KKLZ model was in good agreement with the NPT data. The fitted parameters were $k = 0$ and $\sigma = 0$, which reasonably indicated that the NPT bulk system did not have the effect of the surface field and the quenched disorder. However, the fitting to the NVT bulk system yielded the parameters $k = 1.1$ and $\sigma = 0.7$. This seemed to mean that there were confinement effects, which was not correct. This implies that the KKLZ model is not a perfect model for the system with constant density. Therefore, only the relative difference of these parameters would be considered and used to quantify the effect of the surface field and the quenched disorder. We used the KKLZ model in NVT ensemble was because all the confined systems were in the NVT ensemble due to the technical reasons stated in the session 2 of simulation details.

Figure 3 showed the orientational orders for the five LC systems and the predictions of the KKLZ model. At T = 1.9, the order of the S10 was ∼ 0.3 and apparently bigger than that of the Bulk ∼ 0.08. The bigger order was called the surface induced ordering or paranematic ordering [12, 52–56]. It could be detected by the increase of the fitting parameter of the surface field σ as well. The S10 imposed an extra surface field $\Delta\sigma$ = 1.3–0.7 = 0.6 with respect to the Bulk. As a contrast, the order parameters of RW1 and

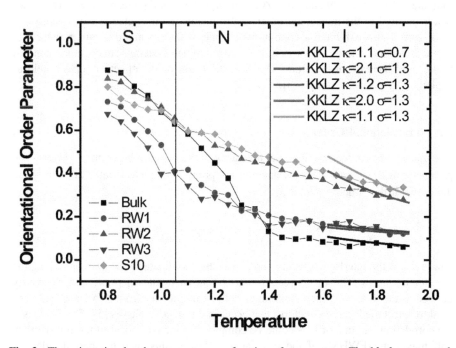

Fig. 3. The orientational order parameter as a function of temperature. The black square, red circle, green up-triangle, blue down-triangle and cyan diamond denoted the simulation data for the systems of Bulk, RW1, RW2, RW3 and S10 respectively. The orientational order of the confined systems, RW1, RW2, RW3 and S10, showed higher orientational order parameters in the isotropic phase. The parameters also evolved continuously in contrast to the transition at T = 1.4 for the Bulk. The change resulted from the effect of the surfaced field [12, 53, 54]. The lines: black, red, green, blue and cyan were the fittings of the KKLZ model for the five systems accordingly. The fitting covered the temperatures ranged from 1.6 to 1.9. The fitted parameter κ and σ were listed as well. The S10 imposed an extra surface field $\Delta\sigma$ = 1.3–0.7 = 0.6 with respect to the Bulk. Compared to the S10, the parameter of the quenched disorder κ exerted by RW1, RW2 and RW3 were $\Delta\kappa$ = 2.1–1.1 = 1, 1.2–1.1 = 0.1 and 2.0–1.1 = 0.9 respectively. These parameters quantitatively exhibited the effect of surface field and quenched disorder (Color figure online).

RW3 were ~ 0.12, which was higher than that of the Bulk but lower than that of the S10. This implied that the quenched disorder disfavored the paranematic ordering. This was represented also by the fitting parameter of the quenched disorder k. With respect to the S10, the effects of QD exerted by RW1 and RW3 were $\Delta k = 2.1 - 1.1 = 1$ and $2.0 - 1.1 = 0.9$, respectively.

Interestingly, the intensity of the QD effect depended on the magnitude of roughness. First, the lower the roughness, the smaller the QD effect. The roughness of RW2 ~ 1.12 was the lowest among the three rough cylinders. Then Δk of RW2 is only 0.1 and smaller than that of RW1 and RW3 which were ~ 1. Second, the more similar the roughness, the more similar the QD effect. RW1 and RW3 had almost the same roughness: SD were 2.79 and 2.88. Δk of them were 1 and 0.9 respectively. These two trends occured to the translation order, the diffusion and the rotation equivalently.

Figure 3 also exhibited a continuous change of the orientational order at the isotropic to nematic phase (I-N) transition for the confined systems. This is in the contrast to the mild increase of the Bulk. This was the result of the effect of surface field as explained by previous study [43].

3.2 Translational Order

The translational order described the regularity of the distance between LC layers. The parameter of the order τ was calculated as the point, which was located at $q* = \frac{2\pi}{d}$, on the curve of the structure factor S_s:

$$\tau = S_s(q* = \frac{2\pi}{d}) = | < \exp(i\frac{2\pi}{d} z_i) >_i | \tag{4}$$

where d was the interlayer spacing and z_i was the coordinate of the particle i along the director of layers. The interlayer spacing d was an unknown priori and rigorously defined as the distance which maximizes τ. The τ might vary from 0 to 1 and had been used to detect the layered structures that occur in the smectic phases [57, 58]. Besides τ, the correlation length ξ of LCs could be computed as the reciprocal of the full width at half maximum (FWHM) of the peak at $q *$ [59]. ξ illustrated the periodic density modulation of the LCs layers.

Figure 4 showed the translational order τ and the correlation lengths ξ of the simulated systems as a function of temperature. In (a), a sharp transition of τ was found at T = 1.05 for the Bulk system which indicated the system evolved from the nematic phase to the smectic phase (N-S) [25, 60]. The transition was not only broadened in S10 and RW2 but also delayed in RW1 and RW3. These observations were in agreement with previous reports [6, 31, 41, 42, 61]. The broadening and the delaying were the results of the effect of the surface field and the quenched disorder respectively. The parameter of RW2 finally reached a value, which was similar to that of S10 at T = 0.85. This could be the regaining of the order in the low disorder condition as predicted by Bellini [2]. The parameters of S10 and RW2 at T = 0.85 were $\sim 55 \%$ lower than that of Bulk and $\sim 20 \%$ higher than those of RW1 and RW3. This implied

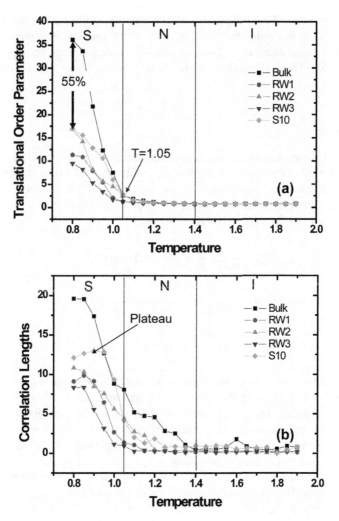

Fig. 4. Temperature variation of the translational order parameter (a) and the correlation length (b). In (a), the translational order of S10 at T = 0.8 was ∼ 17 and ∼ 55 % lower than that of Bulk. The order decreaseed further to ∼ 10 for RW1 and RW3 after the introduction of the quenched disorder. The transition temperature from nematic phase to crystal phase shifted slightly from 1.05 to 1 for RW1 and RW3. In (b), the correlation length of S10 reached a plateau in the smectic phase (T < 0.9) while that of the Bulk increased continuously. The length of RW1 and RW3 reached plateau as well, but at relatively lower temperature and smaller magnitude.

that the effect of the surface field decreased the translational order, which was further decreased by the effect of quenched disorder.

It has been predicted that under confinements, the correlation length ξ of the smectic LCs is finite [2, 58, 61]. The present study proved the prediction by quantitative data as shown in Fig. 4(b). The ξ of S10 reached a plateau in the smectic phase

(T < 1.05) while that of the bulk increased continuously. This was due to the effect of the surface field. It was found that the ξ of RW1, RW3 were less than that of S10. This was attributed to the effect of QD, which had been reported via both experiment and theory [2, 3, 62]. The ξ of the Bulk existed in the nematic phase and this might be the ordering fluctuation.

3.3   Diffusion

The dynamics of the LC particles has been characterized by two standard quantities: the rotational correlation time τ_R and the diffusion coefficient D of mass center [42, 45, 63, 64]. For the diffusion, an extreme anisotropy had been found for the nematic phase in the directions which were parallel or perpendicular to the orientational order [27, 48].

The diffusion coefficients were calculated as:

$$D_{all} = \frac{1}{6} \lim_{t \to \infty} \frac{d}{dt} < [r(t + t_0) - r(t_0)]^2 > \tag{5}$$

$$D_{//} = \frac{1}{4} \lim_{t \to \infty} \frac{d}{dt} < [r_{//}(t + t_0) - r_{//}(t_0)]^2 > \tag{6}$$

$$D_{\perp} = \frac{1}{2} \lim_{t \to \infty} \frac{d}{dt} < [r_{\perp}(t + t_0) - r_{\perp}(t_0)]^2 > \tag{7}$$

where $r(t_0)$ and $r(t + t_0)$ were the vectors of one LC particle at time t_0 and $t + t_0$ respectively; $r_{//}$ and $r_{\perp}$ were the parallel and perpendicular components of r, with $r = r_{//} + r_{\perp}$; and D_{all}, $D_{//}$ and $D_{\perp}$ denoted respectively the diffusion coefficient on average, parallel and perpendicular to the orientational order, which was Z-axis in our systems. The three coefficients of diffusion were calculated for the sake of understanding the effect of QD on the anisotropy.

Figure 5 summarized the anisotropy of the diffusion at different temperatures and compared it with the affine transformation model [65–68]. In (a)–(c), the diffusion coefficients for the Bulk, S10 and RW1 were shown respectively. As found in previous studies, the $D_{//}$ and $D_{\perp}$ for the Bulk were equal to each other in the isotropic phase and splited into different values in the nematic phase [24, 27, 45, 69–71]. The largest anisotropy appeared at T = 1.2 with $D_{//}$ = 0.7 and $D_{\perp}$ = 0.2. Their difference ΔD was 0.5. When T < 1.2, $D_{//}$ decreased and finally merged into the $D_{\perp}$. As shown in (a), the entire profile of the anisotropy was a circle. The characteristics of the anisotropy in the nematic and smectic phase were captured by S10 as well. However, in the isotropic phase, the anisotropy of S10 already existed, due to the high orientational order induced by the surface field as shown in Fig. 3. The largest anisotropy ΔD = 0.8 appeard at T = 1.9 with $D_{//}$ = 1.0 and $D_{\perp}$ = 0.2. For RW1, ΔD = 0.25 appeard at T = 1.9 with $D_{//}$ = 0.55 and $D_{\perp}$ = 0.3. The characteristics of RW2 and RW3 were similar to those of S10 and RW1 respectively. Therefore, the anisotropy of the diffusion was increased by the surface field and decreased by the quenched disorder. And the temperature of the largest anisotropy was shifted from T = 1.2 for the Bulk to T = 1.9 for the S10 and RW1.

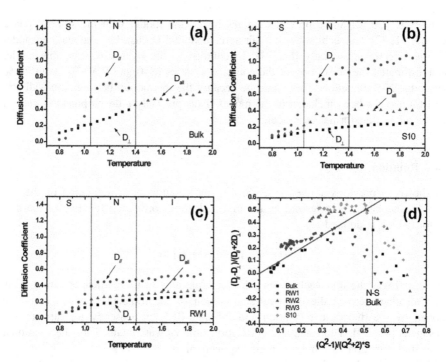

Fig. 5. Diffusivity of the liquid crystal particles. Figure (a)–(c) were diffusion coefficients for the Bulk, S10 and RW1. They showed the average diffusion coefficients D_{all} and also the bias diffusion coefficients: parallel to layers $D_{\parallel}$ and perpendicular to layers $D_{\perp}$. In (a), no anisotropy was found in the isotropic phase $T > 1.4$. As temperature decreased and entered nematic range, diffusion coefficients splited into $D_{\parallel}$ and $D_{\perp}$. $D_{\parallel}$ experienced an increase and then a decrease. Finally, $D_{\parallel}$ merged into $D_{\perp}$ in the smectic phase $T < 1.0$. Figure (b) and (c) exhibited the similar pattern to that of the Bulk, except for the anisotropy in the isotropic phase, which was caused by the surfaced induced order (see Fig. 3). Figure (d) was the anisotropy of diffusion coefficient as a function of the shape scaled order parameter. In (d), the affine transformation model predicted the linear anisotropy of diffusion as the red line showed [65]. The linear trend agreed approximately with the evolution of the Bulk system till the system entered the smectic phase after N-S transition. In the smectic phase, however, there was a significant overestimation of the model. The model also underestimated the anisotropy of the confined system: RW1, RW2, RW3 and S10 by ~ 25 % before the N-S transition.

The affine transformation model is a popular model for predicting the anisotropy of diffusion for the rod-like molecules [65–68, 71–73]. In Fig. 5(d), the model was compared with the simulation data. As shown by the bold red line, the model predicted the linear relationship between the anisotropy of the diffusion and a combination of the orientation order S and the axis ratio $Q = c/a$. A good agreement was found between the Bulk and the model in the isotropic phase and nematic phase, which was in accordance with previous studies [66, 71]. However, after the N-S transition, the anisotropy shrank. This was because that the $D^{\parallel}$ decreased quickly in the smectic phase as shown in (a)–(c). This change was not covered by the model yet, which overestimated the anisotropy as high as 300 %. Some previous studies linked the model with the smectic phase [66–68, 71, 72]. Cinacchi showed a fair agreement and Dvinskikh used another model for the smectic phase only [66, 71]. In contrast to the overestimation, this model underestimated the anisotropy of the confined systems (S10 and RW1-3) about 25 % before the N-S transition. This might be because the interaction between the wall and the LCs had not been included in the model. Thus probably a development is needed for the affine transformation model.

3.4   Rotation

As shown in previous studies [43, 48, 49], the rotation or reorientation of the LC particles has been characterized by the first rank time correlation function of the unit vector, which is defined as:

$$C(t) = <\mathbf{u}(t + t_0)\mathbf{u}(t_0)> \tag{8}$$

where $u(t)$ was the unit vector along the principle axis of the particle at time t. This function characterized the end-over-end motion of the molecules, which could be probed by the dielectric relaxation and infrared (IR) spectroscopy for dipolar real mesogens [42, 74]. The rotational correlation time τ_R was obtained for the rotational correlation function assuming a single exponential decay.

The rotational correlation time τ_R was shown in Fig. 6. For the bulk system, an apparent slope variation occured at the I-N transition. A second almost Arrhenius behavior with a much larger activation energy was observed in the nematic and smectic phases. The phenomena had been found by Bates also [75]. The slope variation might be due to the loss of the local free volume at the nematic phase. Different from the slope change, those confined GB systems displayed a unique Arrhenius behavior on the entire temperature range studied. It was related to the continuous I-N transition in the confined systems. As for the rough cylinders, τ_R for the RW1 and RW3 was slightly smaller than that for S10. The difference increased as temperature decreased. These indicated that under the effect of QD, the rotation in the rough cylinders was easier than that in the smooth cylinder. This was because that the rough cylinders had lower orientational order (see Fig. 3), which provided larger local free volume and then loosens the reduction of the rotation partially.

The rotational motion has been related to the layered structure in the smectic phase [76]. However, at the N-S phase transition in Fig. 6, the present simulation data only showed the continuous increase of τ_R. As suggested by Allen, there are two rotation modes in the smectic phase [76]. First, a LC particle escape from a layer and enters the interlayer region. After some time, the particle returns the original layer. Second, a LC particle rotates within the layer. The first mode is the major mode of the rotation by the virtue of the extremely high energy barrier of the second mode [76]. In this study, the rotation of the first mode was still rare because the rotation mode depends directly on the probability of the particle sitting at interlayer region [76]. The probability was related to the length-to-breadth ratio which is 4.4 in this study. When the ratio increased from 3.8 to 5.0, the probability decreased from 0.016 to 0.000017.77. Therefore, the

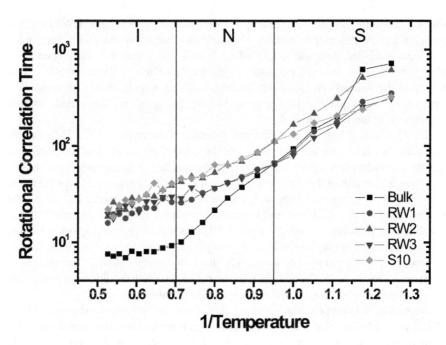

Fig. 6. Temperature variation of the rotational correlation time τ_R. τ_R increased as temperature decreased. τ_R of S10 was three times longer than that of Bulk and slightly longer than those of the rough cylinders RW1 and RW3 at $1/T = 0.55$. For the Bulk curve, an apparent slope variation occured around $1/T = 0.7$, which was in contrast to the continuous increase of the confined systems RW1, RW2, RW3 and S10. This might be attributed to the continuous I-N transition in the confined systems (see Fig. 3).

probability in this study could be expected to be ~ 0.008 by assuming a linear insertion. With such a low probability, the influence of the layer on the rotation was a very difficult to detect. Therefore, the simulation data only showed the continuous increase of τ_R.

4   Conclusion

The surface field and the quenched disorder (QD) are two key factors associated with the nano-confinement. In order to distinguish the two factors, this paper reported the simulation results of liquid crystals (LCs) under the cylinder confinements and compared the results with the Landau-de Gennes KKLZ model and the affine transformation model.

The quenched disorder was introduced by aperiodical rough cylinders which were first constructed via the idea of spherical indentation. This method greatly avoided the periodicity in previous methods and kept the equivalent features with the experiments. The method produced three aperiodic rough cylinders: RW1, RW2 and RW3. The magnitude of roughness of the three cylinders was RW1 $\approx$ RW3 > RW2.

Simulation results showed the similarity between the system RW1 and RW3 in all the structural and the dynamic properties. This indicated that the systems with comparable roughness exhibited comparable QD effect. It was also found that the properties of RW2 were closer to those of the smooth cylinder than those of RW1 and RW3. This illustrated the intensity of QD effect depended on the magnitude of roughness. The conclusions were quantitatively proved by the fitting of the quenched disorder parameter κ in the KKLZ model.

The QD affected both the structure and dynamics of the confined LCs. The structure was analyzed via the orientational order and the translational order. Under the effect of QD, the two orders of rough cylinders were lower than that of the smooth cylinder. And the correlation length of the translational order also showed a lower value for the rough cylinders. Thus, QD reduced the structure ordering of the confined LCs. As for the dynamics, diffusion coefficients and rotational correlation time were presented. It was found that the anisotropy of the diffusion coefficients was as high as 0.8 for the smooth cylinder while that of rough cylinders were only 0.25. The rotational correlation time of the smooth cylinder was slightly longer than that of the rough cylinder. The elongation increased as temperature decreased. Therefore, QD lessened the diffusion anisotropy and shortened the rotational correlation time of the confined LCs.

Interesting information was further gathered for the anisotropic diffusion of the LCs. It is well known that LCs in the nematic phase possess obvious anisotropy. That is, the diffusion coefficient parallel to the layer $D_{//}$ is different from that perpendicular to the layer $D_{\perp}$. In this paper, $D_{//}$ exhibited an increase and then a decrease as the temperature cooled. $D_{//}$ finally merged with $D_{\perp}$ after LCs enterd the smectic phase. So the entire pattern of the anisotropic diffusion was a circle. On the other hand, the simulation results validated the prediction of the anisotropy made by the affine transformation model for the Bulk system in the isotropic and the nematic phases. However, the prediction overestimated the anisotropy in the smectic phase and underestimated the anisotropy for the confined system. Therefore, a development of the model might needed.

Acknowledgements. I thank Dr. Ronan Lefort and Dr. Denis Morineau (Institute of Physics of Rennes, C.N.R.S -University of Rennes 1, FRANCE) for the idea initiation and helpful discussion. This study was part of the post-doctoral fellowship project of Qing Ji, supported by a grant from the C.N.R.S.

References

1. Wu, Y.Y., Cheng, G.S., Katsov, K., Sides, S.W., Wang, J.F., Tang, J., Fredrickson, G.H., Moskovits, M., Stucky, G.D.: Nat. Mater. **3**, 816–822 (2004)
2. Bellini, T., Radzihovsky, L., Toner, J., Clark, N.A.: Science **294**, 1074–1079 (2001)
3. Liang, D., Borthwick, M.A., Leheny, R.L.: J. Phys.-Condens. Matter **16**, S1989–S2002 (2004)
4. Clegg, P.S.: Acta Crystallogr. Sect. A **61**, 112–121 (2005)
5. Bellini, T., Chiccoli, C., Pasini, P., Zannoni, C.: Phys. Rev. E **54**, 2647–2652 (1996)

6. Clegg, P.S., Stock, C., Birgeneau, R.J., Garland, C.W., Roshi, A., Iannacchione, G.S.: Phys. Rev. E **67**, 021703–021716 (2003)
7. Ramazanoglu, M., Larochelle, S., Garland, C.W., Birgeneau, R.J.: Phys. Rev. E **77**, 031702–031712 (2008)
8. Sharma, D.: Liq. Cryst. **35**, 1215–1224 (2008)
9. Zhang, Z.P., Chakrabarti, A.: Phys. Rev. E **52**, 4991–4999 (1995)
10. Iannacchione, G.S., Crawford, G.P., Qian, S., Doane, J.W., Finotello, D.: Phys. Rev. E **53**, 2402–2411 (1996)
11. Kityk, A.V., Wolff, M., Knorr, K., Morineau, D., Lefort, R., Huber, P.: Phys. Rev. Lett. **101**, 187801–187804 (2008)
12. Crawford, G.P., Stannarius, R., Doane, J.W.: Phys. Rev. A **44**, 2558–2569 (1991)
13. Liang, D., Leheny, R.L.: Phys. Rev. E **75**, 031705–031716 (2007)
14. Huairen Zeng, B.Z., Iannacchione, G.S., Finotello, D.: Phys. Rev. E **60**, 5607–5618 (1999)
15. Park, S., Leheny, R.L., Birgeneau, R.J., Gallani, J.L., Garland, C.W., Iannacchione, G.S.: Phys. Rev. E **65**, 050703–050707 (2002)
16. Kutnjak, Z., Kralj, S., Lahajnar, G., Zumer, S.: Phys. Rev. E **68**, 021705–021717 (2003)
17. Caggioni, M., Roshi, A., Barjami, S., Mantegazza, F., Iannacchione, G.S., Bellini, T.: Phys. Rev. Lett. **93**, 127801–127805 (2004)
18. Roshi, A., Iannacchione, G.S., Clegg, P.S., Birgeneau, R.J.: Phys. Rev. E **69**, 031703–031714 (2004)
19. Sharma, D., Iannacchione, G.: J. Phys. Chem. B **111**, 1916–1922 (2007)
20. Sharma, D.: J. Therm. Anal. Calorim. **93**, 899–906 (2008)
21. Gelb, L.D., Gubbins, K.E., Radhakrishnan, R., Sliwinska-Bartkowiak, M.: Rep. Prog. Phys. **62**, 1573–1659 (1999)
22. Kralj, S., Popa-Nita, V.: Eur. Phys. J. E **14**, 115–125 (2004)
23. Kralj, S., Cordoyiannis, G., Zidansek, A., Lahajnar, G., Amenitsch, H., Zumer, S., Kutnjak, Z.: J. Chem. Phys. **127**, 154905–1549014 (2007)
24. Busselez, R., Ecolivet, C., Guegan, R., Lefort, R., Morineau, D., Toudic, B., Guendouz, M., Affouard, F.: Int. J. Nanotechnol. **5**, 867–884 (2008)
25. Bates, M.A., Luckhurst, G.R.: J. Chem. Phys. **110**, 7087–7108 (1999)
26. De Miguel, E., Blas, F.J., Del Rio, E.M.: Mol. Phys. **104**, 2919–2927 (2006)
27. Mima, T., Yasuoka, K.: Phys. Rev. E **77**, 011705–011716 (2008)
28. Quintana, J., Poire, E.C., Dominguez, H., Alejandre, J.: Mol. Phys. **100**, 2597–2604 (2002)
29. Wall, G.D., Cleaver, D.J.: Mol. Phys. **101**, 1105–1112 (2003)
30. Bellier-Castella, L., Caprion, D., Ryckaert, J.P.: J. Chem. Phys. **121**, 4874–4883 (2004)
31. Steuer, H., Hess, S., Schoen, M.: Phys. Rev. E **69**, 031708 (2004)
32. de las Heras, D., Velasco, E., Mederos, L.: Phys. Rev. Lett. **94**, 017801–017804 (2005)
33. Cleaver, D.J., Allen, M.P.: Mol. Phys. **80**, 253–276 (1993)
34. Cheung, D.L., Schmid, F.: Chem. Phys. Lett. **418**, 392–396 (2006)
35. Cheung, D.L., Schmid, F.: J. Chem. Phys. **122**, 074902–074909 (2005)
36. Jabbarzadeh, A., Atkinson, J.D., Tanner, R.I.: Phys. Rev. E **61**, 690–699 (2000)
37. Coasne, B., Pellenq, R.J.M.: J. Chem. Phys. **120**, 2913–2922 (2004)
38. Kuchta, B., Firlej, L., Boulet, P., Marzec, M.: Appl. Surf. Sci. **253**, 5596–5600 (2007)
39. Kuchta, B., Firlej, L., Denoyel, R., Boulet, P., Rols, S., Johnson, M.R.: Appl. Surf. Sci. **253**, 5601–5605 (2007)
40. Strickland, B., Leptoukh, G., Roland, C.: J. Phys. a-Math. Gen. **28**, L403–L408 (1995)
41. Guegan, R., Morineau, D., Loverdo, C., Beziel, W., Guendouz, M.: Phys. Rev. E **73**, 011707–011713 (2006)
42. Guegan, R., Morineau, D., Lefort, R., Moreac, A., Beziel, W., Guendouz, M., Zanotti, J.M., Frick, B.: J. Chem. Phys. **126**, 064902–064912 (2007)

43. Ji, Q., Lefort, R., Busselez, R., Morineau, D.: J. Chem. Phys. **130**, 234501–234509 (2009)
44. Gay, J.G., Berne, B.J.: J. Chem. Phys. **74**, 3316–3319 (1981)
45. Bates, M.A., Luckhurst, G.R.: J. Chem. Phys. **120**, 394–403 (2004)
46. Bates, M.A., Luckhurst, G.R.: J. Chem. Phys. **118**, 6605–6614 (2003)
47. de Miguel, E., del Rio, E.M., Blas, F.J.: J. Chem. Phys. **121**, 11183–11194 (2004)
48. Ji, Q., Lefort, R., Ghoufi, A., Morineau, D.: Chem. Phys. Lett. **482**, 234–238 (2009)
49. Ji, Q., Lefort, R., Morineau, D.: Chem. Phys. Lett. **478**, 161–165 (2009)
50. Plimpton, S.: J. Comput. Phys. **117**, 1–19 (1995)
51. Sheng, P.: Phys. Rev. Lett. **37**, 1059–1062 (1976)
52. Gwozdz, E., Pasterny, K., Brodka, A.: Chem. Phys. Lett. **329**, 106–111 (2000)
53. Mima, T., Narumi, T., Kameoka, S., Yasuoka, K.: Mol. Simul. **34**, 761–773 (2008)
54. Wall, G.D., Cleaver, D.J.: Phys. Rev. E **56**, 4306–4316 (1997)
55. de las Heras, D., Velasco, E., Mederos, L.: J. Chem. Phys. **120**, 4949–4957 (2004)
56. Zhou, X., Chen, H., Iwamoto, M.: J. Chem. Phys. **120**, 5322–5326 (2004)
57. Fisch, R.: Phys. Rev. B **58**, 5684–5691 (1998)
58. Lambreva, D.M., Ostrovskii, B.I., Finkelmann, H., de Jeu, W.H.: Phys. Rev. Lett. **93**, 185702–185706 (2004)
59. Fan, Z.X.S., Seguel, C.G., Aguilera, C., Haase, W.: Liq. Cryst. **11**, 401–409 (1992)
60. De miguel, E., Rull, L.F., Chalam, M.K., Gubbins, K.E.: Mol. Phys. **74**, 405–424 (1991)
61. Larochelle, S., Ramazanoglu, M., Birgeneau, R.J.: Phys. Rev. E **73**, 060702–060706 (2006)
62. Bellini, T., Clark, N.A., Muzny, C.D., Wu, L., Garland, C.W., Schaefer, D.W., Olivier, B.J., Oliver, B.J.: Phys. Rev. Lett. **69**, 788–791 (1992)
63. Chakrabarti, D., Bagchi, B.: J. Phys. Chem. B **111**, 11646–11657 (2007)
64. Giacomo, P., De Gaetani, L., Alessandro, T.: J. Chem. Phys. **128**, 194501–194512 (2008)
65. Hess, S., Frenkel, D., Allen, M.P.: Mol. Phys. **74**, 765–774 (1991)
66. Dvinskikh, S.V., Furo, I., Zimmermann, H., Maliniak, A.: Phys. Rev. E **65**, 061701–061710 (2002)
67. Cifelli, M., Cinacchi, G., De Gaetani, L.: J. Chem. Phys. **125**, 164912–164919 (2006)
68. Grelet, E., Lettinga, M.P., Bier, M., van Roij, R., van der Schoot, P.: J. Phys.-Condens. Matter **20**, 494213–494219 (2008)
69. Demiguel, E., Rull, L.F., Gubbins, K.E.: Phys. Rev. A **45**, 3813–3822 (1992)
70. Dieter, S.H.: Baalss. Physical Review Letters **57**, 86–89 (1986)
71. Cinacchi, G., De Gaetani, L., Tani, A.: J. Chem. Phys. **122**, 184513–184522 (2005)
72. Lettinga, M.P., Grelet, E.: Phys. Rev. Lett. **99**, 197802–197806 (2007)
73. Kroger, M.: Phys. Rep.-Rev. Sec. Phys. Lett. **390**, 453–551 (2004)
74. Morineau, D., Lefort, R., Guégan, R., Guendouz, M., Zanotti, J.M., Bernhard, F.: Phys. Rev. E **78**, 040701–040705 (2008)
75. Bates, M.A., Luckhurst, G.R.: Mol. Phys. **99**, 1365–1371 (2001)
76. Van Duijneveldt, J.S., Allen, M.P.: Mol. Phys. **90**, 243–250 (1997)

Visual Tracking Based on Convolutional Deep Belief Network

Dan Hu[1,3], Xingshe Zhou[1], and Junjie Wu[2(✉)]

[1] School of Computer Science, Northwestern Polytechnical University, Xi'an, China
[2] State Key Laboratory of High Performance Computing,
National University of Defense Technology, Changsha, China
junjiewu@nudt.edu.cn
[3] Information and Navigation College,
Air Force Engineering University, Xi'an, China

Abstract. Visual tracking is an important task within the field of computer vision. Recently, deep neural networks have gained significant attention thanks to their success on learning image features. But the existing deep neural networks applied in visual tracking are full-connected complicated architectures with large amount of redundant parameters that would be low efficiently to learn. We tackle this problem by using a novel convolutional deep belief network (CDBN) with convolution, weights sharing and pooling to have much fewer parameters to learn, in addition to gain translation invariance which would benefit the tracker performance. Theoretical analysis and experimental evaluations on an open tracker benchmark demonstrate our CDBN based tracker is more accurate by improving tracking success rate 22.6 % and tracking precision 62.8 % on average, while maintaining low computation cost by reduces the number of parameters to 44.4 %, compared to DLT, another well-known deep learning tracker. Meanwhile, our tracker can achieve real-time performance by a graphics processing unit (GPU) speedup of 2.61 times on average and up to 3.08 times.

Keywords: Visual tracking · Deep learning · Convolutional deep belief network · GPU

1 Introduction

Visual tracking is a fundamental problem in computer vision. In most existing trackers, even those reporting satisfactory results, features are manually defined and combined [1,2], which may not be good enough for object tracking in harsh nature [3,4], due to the limitations of prior knowledge about the object and the complex environments.

Over the last two years, deep learning, which are machine learning algorithms inspired by brains, based on learning multiple levels of representation, have achieved an impressive suite of results thanks to their success on automatic

© Springer International Publishing Switzerland 2015
Y. Chen et al. (Eds.): APPT 2015, LNCS 9231, pp. 103–115, 2015.
DOI: 10.1007/978-3-319-23216-4_8

feature extraction via multi-layer nonlinear transformations, especially in computer vision [5,6], speech recognition [7,8] and natural language processing [9]. However, the application of deep learning in visual tracking is less explored. The reason is, in the case of visual tracking, we typically have only very few positive instances extracted from the first video frame for training (in fact mostly we only have one single labeled example), which makes the direct applying of the deep learning approaches infeasible.

In this paper, we employ the Convolutional Deep Belief Networks (CDBN) [10], an extension of the DBNs [11,12], as a generic image feature extractor being offline pre-trained and then transfer its rich feature hierarchies into online tracking to overcome this problem. Our proposed method is inspired by the deep learning tracker (DLT) [13], the first work on applying deep neural networks that is a Stacked Denoising Autoencoder (SDAE) [14], to visual tracking, and has reported encouraging results, but they are quite different. The main contributions of this work include:

1. To our knowledge, this work is the first time a CDBN is applied to visual tracking. Theoretical analysis demonstrates it can improve training efficiency by reducing the number of parameters to 44.4 % of those in DLT, which need to learn and fine-tune by expensive computation during the offline pre-training and online tracking stages.
2. We evaluate the tracking accuracy of our proposed method on one open tracker benchmark [15], and experiment results outperform DLT by improving tracking success rate and tracking precision on an average of 22.6 % and 62.8 %, correspondingly.
3. Thanks to a very efficient GPU parallel implementation of the convolution operation, our tracker achieves a speedup of 2.61 times on average, up to 3.08 times, which is sufficient for many real-time applications.

The rest of this paper is organized as follows: Sect. 2 describes the details of our CDBN tracking algorithm. Section 3 presents theoretical analysis and experimental evaluation results and Sect. 4 summarizes the conclusion.

2 Our Approach

The basic idea of our method is that: In the first place, we employ a large dataset to offline pre-train a CDBN to extract rich feature hierarchies, and then we transfer the learned features to the online tracking tasks to distinguish the tracked object from its surrounding background. The online tracking process will select the region with the highest score, which is the output of a softmax classifier on top of the CDBN, as the new location of the object based on a particle filter framework. We update the whole CDBN model in a lazy manner only when significant appearance change happens.

2.1   The Dataset

Tiny Images [16] is a dataset of 79 million unique 32×32 color images gathered from the Internet. Each image is loosely labeled with one of 75,062 English nouns, which covers all visual object classes. The samples from this dataset are shown in Fig. 1. 1st & 3rd columns are four 32×32 resolution color images. Despite their low resolution, it is still possible to recognize most of the objects and scenes. 2nd & 4th columns are collages showing the 16 nearest neighbors within the dataset to each image in the adjacent column. Note the consistency between the neighbors and the query image, having related objects in similar spatial arrangements. So the dataset contains more copious and abundant amount of images. In [17], the authors experimentally probe that pre-training with such training data, would benefit and lead to a large improvement in detection performance. All of these motivate our choice of these low resolution images which can effectively reduce computational complexity.

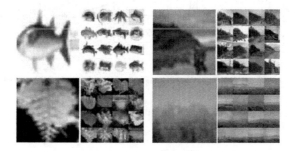

Fig. 1. Image samples from tiny image dataset [16].

We randomly sample 1 million images from this dataset with 256 classes as the inputs of our CDBN model to pre-train it to be a generic feature extractor. We did not pre-process the images in any other way, except for scaling the raw pixels to the range $[0, 1]$ linearly.

2.2   Our CDBN Model

Now we are ready to describe the overall architecture of our own CDBN which would be constructed as a generic feature extractor and then be transfered its rich feature hierarchies into our online tracking framework. Analogously to DBNs, the Convolutional Deep Belief Networks consist of several Convolutional Restricted Boltzman Machines (CRBMs) stacked on top of another. Inspired by the local receptive fields and shared weights mechanisms of the CNNs [18], the connections between the hidden and the visible layers are local (instead of full-connected) and weights are shared among all locations in an image.

As depicted in Fig. 2, our CDBN contains two convolutional layers, corresponding sigmoid functions as activation function and max-pooling operators.

The input to the CDBNs visible layer is locally normalized 32×32 image patches. The first convolutional layer filters the input image with 10 kernels of size 9×9, and the second convolutional layer takes as input the output of the first convolutional layer and filters it with 16 kernels of size 5×5. All these kernels scan each image in the previous layer, and one kernel shares one set of weight vectors for all different images to extract one type of feature. The max-pooling operators over the local neighborhoods reduce the resolution from the feature maps derived by the former convolution operators. The fully-connected layer is connected to all neurons in the previous layer, and the output of the full-connected layer is fed to a 256-way softmax which produces a distribution over the 256 class labels. Thus, the number of neurons in the networks remaining layers is given by 32×32 - $24 \times 24 \times 10$ -$12 \times 12 \times 10$ - $8 \times 8 \times 160$ - $4 \times 4 \times 160$ - 1024 - 256 -1.

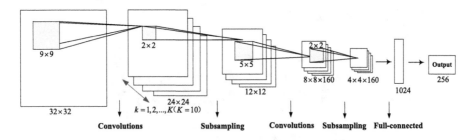

Fig. 2. Architecture of our CDBN.

Our model is governed by the energy function as in Eq. (1):

$$P(v,c) = \frac{1}{Z} \exp(-E(v,c)),$$

$$E(v,c) = -\sum_{k=1}^{K} \sum_{i,j=1}^{N_C} \sum_{r,s=1}^{N_W} c_{ij}^k W_{rs}^k v_{i+r-1,j+s-1}$$

$$-\sum_{i,j=1}^{N_V} b_k \sum_{i,j=1}^{N_C} c_{ij}^k - b_v \sum_{i,j=1}^{N_V} v_{ij} + \frac{1}{2} \sum_{i,j=1}^{N_V} v_{ij}^2,$$

$$s.t. \quad \sum_{(i,j) \in B_\alpha} c_{i,j}^k \leq 1, \quad \forall k, \alpha. \tag{1}$$

Here, v and c are visible and convolutional units correspondingly. Each convolution kernel has a bias $b_k (k = 1, 2, ...K)$ and all visible units share a single bias b_v. W_{rs}^k are the weights between a convolution node in the kth feature map and the visible nodes, $c_{i,j}^k$ are locally neighboring hidden units in the kth feature map that are max-pooled to a pooling node p_α^k and B_α refers to the block of them.

As with standard RBMs, the conditional probabilities can be computed using block Gibbs sampling as in Eq. (2) [19]:

$$P(c_{i,j}^k = 1|v) = \frac{\exp\left(I(c_{i,j}^k)\right)}{1 + \sum\limits_{(i',j') \in B_\alpha} \exp\left(I(c_{i',j'}^k)\right)},$$

$$P(v_{ij} = 1|c) = \mathbb{N}((\sum_k W^k *_f c^k)_{ij} + b_v, 1). \tag{2}$$

Where $I(c_{i,j}^k) \triangleq b_k + (\tilde{W}^k *_v v)_{ij}$, $\mathbb{N}(\cdot)$ is a normal distribution, $\tilde{W}$ refers to rotating the original convolution kernel W in $180°$, $*_v$ stands for valid convolution operation, and $*_f$ stands for full convolution operation.

The posterior distribution of the pooling node p_α^k which is defined as $p_\alpha^k \triangleq \sum\limits_{(i,j) \in B_\alpha} c_{i,j}^k$ can be defined as in Eq. (3):

$$P(p_\alpha^k = 1|v) = \frac{\sum\limits_{(i',j') \in B_\alpha} \exp(I(c_{i',j'}^k))}{1 + \sum\limits_{(i',j') \in B_\alpha} \exp(I(c_{i',j'}^k))}. \tag{3}$$

After constructing a convolutional deep belief network, we pretain layer-by-layer followed by unrolling it to form a feedforward neural network. Afterward, the whole network is fine-tuned using contrastive divergence optimization algorithm.

2.3   Online Tracking

Inspired by the work of Wang et al. [13], our visual tracking algorithm is also carried out based on a particle filter framework, which is a sequential Monte Carlo importance sampling method for estimating the latent state variables of a dynamical system based on a sequence of observations [20, 21].

In the first frame, the object to track has been provided by the bounding box. Then the object region and the surrounding regions are regarded as positive sample and negative samples correspondingly, which are used to fine-tune the CDBN to adapt to the appearance of object in the first frame. When a new video frame arrives, the confidence for each particle is made by the networks softmax by making a simple forward pass through the network.

Instead of updating the CDBN model at each frame, which would be computationally expensive, we propose to update the CDBM in a lazy manner, only when the maximum confidence of all particles in a frame is below a predefined threshold, which indicates significant appearance change of the object being tracked occurs. This method accelerates our tracking algorithm exceedingly on the reason that the appearance of the object is not always changing in adjacent frames, our CDBN model can remain discriminant until significant appearance change happens.

3   Theoretical Analysis and Experimental Evaluation

3.1   Baseline

In Sect. 3, we first simply theoretical analyze the training efficiency of our CDBN compared to the full-connected SDAE used in DLT tracker, which is the first attempt of deep learning for tracing, and its architecture is illustrated in Fig. 3.

Then we evaluate the performance of our proposed method on a recently released benchmark [15], which is the largest open dataset consisting of 50 fully annotated sequences and attributes, to facilitate tracking evaluation. These attributes are defined by the factors that affect tracking performance, such as occlusion, fast motion, and illumination variation. We compare our CDBN tracker with some state-of-art trackers, including DLT, TLD [22], MIL [23], IVT [24], CT [25], and VTD [26].

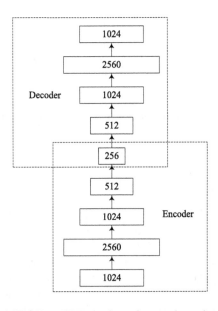

Fig. 3. Architecture of SDAE in DLT tracker, the number of neurons is 1024 - 2560 - 1024 - 512 - 256.

Performances are measured by tracking success rate (TSR) and tracking precision (TP). Tracking success rate is calculated by the percentage of frames in which the overlapping ratio $\pi(k)$ between the estimated location and the ground truth against the entire union box, as defined in Eq. (4), is larger than a given overlapping-threshold, which is 50 % in this paper.

$$\pi(k) = \frac{area(B_k^T \cap B_k^G)}{area(B_k^T \cup B_k^G)}. \tag{4}$$

Where B_k^T is the estimated location bounding box and B_k^G is the ground truth of the kth frame, $\cap$ and $\cup$ denote the intersection and union operations respectively. Tracking precision is defined as the Euclidean distance between the center of B_k^T and the B_k^G in pixels.

3.2   Implementation Details

We run our algorithm in Matlab on a desktop PC with a 3.2 GHz i5 quad core CPU and a NVIDIA GTX750 GPU, by invoking the Matlab parallel computing toolbox to accelerate the computation. We use the contrastive divergence algorithm with momentum for optimization. We start with learning rate of 0.1 with momentum 0.5 and increase it to 0.9 after 5 epochs. We train about 20 epochs in total with the batch size to 100. The threshold for online fine-tuning the whole network is set to 0.8. The particle filter uses 1000 particles in a search window twice to the area of bounding box around the estimated location in last frame. We also run the DLT code[1] on our platform. The results of other trackers are obtained from [15].

3.3   Theoretical Analysis of Convolutional vs. Fully Connected Layer

The SDAE used in DLT tracker is a fully-connected deep learning model, ignoring the topology and correlation of 2D images as need to learn weights separately for every location. However, our CDBN makes use of two convolutional layers before having fully connected layer, as depicted in Fig. 2. The convolutional layers are meant to reduce spatial variation and model spatial correlation, while the fully connected layer aggregates the local information learned in the convolutional layer to do class discrimination. Table 1 shows the number of weight and bias of our net compared to the SDAE.

Table 1. The quantitative comparison of parameter number.

	Weight	Bias	Total
CDBN(Ours)	2,622,650	27	2,622,677
SDAE [13]	5,898,240	5,376	5,903,616

Our CDBN applies convolution and weights sharing mechanism to reduce the number of parameters remarkably to only 44.4 % of the SDAEs. The parameters learning and fine-tuning is so computationally expensive that our method will maintain low computational cost to improve training efficiency exceedingly.

On the other hand, current GPU has pair with a highly-optimized implementation of 2D convolution. Meanwhile, an excellent work has been reported [27]

---

[1] http://winsty.net/dlt.html.

that training of convolutional deep belief networks in the frequency domain demonstrates a speedup of up to 8 times on 2D images. So our model can be learned much more efficiently further.

3.4   Experiment Evaluations

Performances of the 7 tracker over 8 video sequences are summarized in Tables 2 and 3, the best results are highlighted in bold font.

As depicted in Fig. 4, our proposed method achieves the best results compared with other trackers on 4 video sequences. For the other 4 video sequences, ours is also among the best three methods, and all are superior to DLT tracker by an average of 22.6 % on tracking success rate and an average of 62.8 % on tracking precision, correspondingly. The key to this success is the translation invariance gained by weights sharing and pooling mechanisms. In nature, shifts

Table 2. The performance(TSR) comparison of our proposed method and the other visual trackers. The best results in bold font.

	Ours	DLT	TLD	MIL	IVT	CT	VTD
Woman	**73.8**	67.1	5.8	12.2	21.5	16.0	17.1
David3	61.3	33.3	-	**68.3**	63.5	34.9	-
Girl	**79.6**	73.5	-	29.4	18.6	17.8	-
David	68.7	66.1	44.4	17.7	**92.0**	25.3	49.4
Trellis	**95.3**	93.6	48.9	25.9	44.3	23.0	30.1
Singer1	**100**	**100**	53.6	10.3	96.3	10.3	99.4
Shaking	65.2	35.4	15.6	26.0	1.1	92.3	**99.2**
Bolt	33.7	2.3	-	1.1	1.4	0.6	**55.7**
Average	**72.2**	58.9	33.7	23.9	42.3	27.5	58.5

Table 3. The performance(TP) comparison of our proposed method and the other visual trackers. The best results in bold font.

	Ours	DLT	TLD	MIL	IVT	CT	VTD
Woman	**8.9**	9.4	-	123.7	111.2	109.6	133.6
David3	57.9	104.8	-	**29.7**	52.0	88.7	-
Girl	**3.5**	4.0	-	13.7	22.5	18.9	-
David	6.9	7.1	-	13.1	**3.9**	15.3	27.1
Trellis	**3.2**	3.3	48.0	71.7	44.7	80.4	81.3
Singer1	**3.0**	3.3	-	26.0	7.9	16.8	3.4
Shaking	7.5	11.5	-	28.6	138.4	10.9	**5.2**
Bolt	106.8	388.1	-	393.5	397.0	363.8	**14**
Average	**24.7**	66.4	48.0	87.5	97.2	88.1	44.1

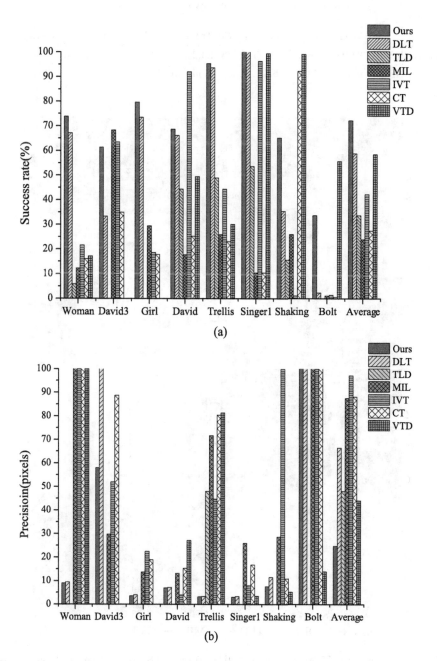

Fig. 4. Histogram for the performance comparison. (a) Tracking success rate (the higher the better); (b) Tracking precision (the lower the better).

Table 4. Running time on 8 video sequences (fps).

	Woman	David3	Girl	David	Trellis	Singer1	Shaking	Bolt	Average
With GPU	24.98	18.01	16.17	19.78	23.25	18.17	19.07	14.03	19.18
No GPU	9.38	7.03	6.32	7.53	7.56	9.45	6.50	5.13	7.36

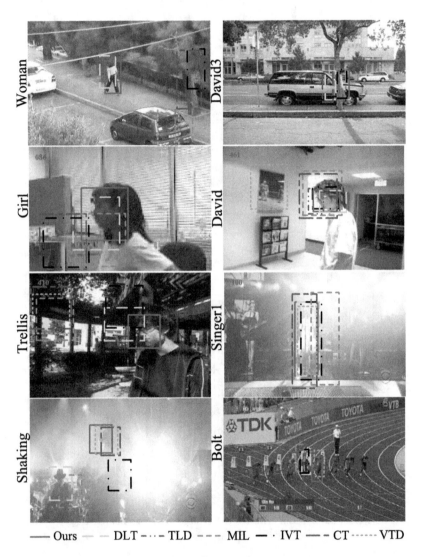

—— Ours — — DLT -···- TLD --- MIL —·— IVT —— CT ······ VTD

Fig. 5. Comparison of 7 trackers on several key frames of 8 video sequences. Woman and david3 are examples of handling occlusions; Girl and david are examples of handling pose changes; Shaking and singer1 are examples of handling illumination changes; Bolt is examples of handling deformation.

or distortions may cause the position of object to vary, which desires the model to incorporate invariance to them. So our algorithm demonstrates better performance in some scenes with occlusions, pose and illumination changes.

Thanks to advances of the GPU technology for the parallel implementation of convolution operation, our tracker can achieve a speedup of 2.61 times on average, up to 3.08 times. In addition, our tracker achieves an average frame rate of 19.18 fps on our platform, as shown in Table 4, which is sufficient for many real-time applications.

Figure 5 shows some key frames with bounding boxes reported by all 7 trackers for each of the 8 video sequences, which present our tolerance to occlusions, pose and illumination changes.

The woman and david3 sequences are challenging for severe occlusions and pose changes. Our tracker doesn't drift for woman whilst most other trackers fail or drift at about frame 550. For david3, our tracker rarely misses the target completely expect full occlusion.

The girl, david, shaking, singer1, and trellis sequences are all arduous since drastical pose changes in addition to illumination vary for the last three. For singer1 and trellis, our method can track the object accurately along the entire sequence. For girl, most trackers drift at about frame 86, while our method can track the girl even after she turns. For david, all trackers drift or even fail to different degrees except for IVT, our tracker yield the second best results. For shaking, VTD and CT give satisfactory results, followed by ours which is much better than DLT.

The Bolt is challenging for the severe deformation, most trackers fail or drift in early frames, and our results are less satisfactory too.

Our tracker shows the promising performance for most video sequences. In addition, the results demonstrate that our tracker and the DLT tracker which all use deep learning models as generic feature extractor, win the most and second most successful tracking. The experimental comparisons suggest the outstanding future for the application of deep learning in visual tracking. Furthermore, our results can be improved simply by waiting for faster GPUs and bigger datasets to become available.

4 Conclusion

We have proposed a novel learning method for visual tracking based on deep neural network. To realize this approach, we first train a CDBN model using an auxiliary Tiny Images dataset to learn generic image feature representation. After that, the output of the CDBN is used to train a softmax classifier to distinguish the object from the background. Then, a particle filter online tracking framework predicts the new location with highest confidence. Theoretical analysis and experimental comparisons demonstrate that deep learning based trackers achieve encouraging results and the convolutional deep belief network shows much more training efficiency and better capability than stacked denoising autoencoder in visual tracking application.

References

1. Adam, A., Rivlin, E., Shimshoni, I.: Robust fragments-based tracking using the integral histogram. In: IEEE Conference on Computer Vision and Pattern Recognition (CVPR) (2006)
2. Hare, S., Saffari, A., Torr, P.H.: Struck: structured output tracking with kernels. In: IEEE International Conference on Computer Vision (ICCV) (2011)
3. Yang, H., Shao, L., Zheng, F., Wang, L., Song, Z.: Recent advances and trends in visual tracking: a review. Neurocomputing **74**(18), 3823–3831 (2011)
4. Smeulders, A., Chu, D., Cucchiara, R., Calderara, S., Dehghan, A., Shah, M.: Visual tracking: an experimental survey. IEEE Trans. Pattern Anal. Mach. Intell. **36**(7), 1442–1468 (2014)
5. Krizhevsky, A., Sutskever, I., Hinton, G.E.: ImageNet classification with deep convolutional neural networks. In: Annual Conference on Neural Information Processing Systems (NIPS) (2012)
6. Donahue, J., Jia, Y., Vinyals, O., Hoffman, J., Zhang, N., Tzeng, E., Darrell, T.: Decaf: A Deep Convolutional Activation Feature for Generic Visual Recognition (2013). arXiv preprint arXiv:1310.1531
7. Hinton, G.E., Deng, L., Yu, D., Dahl, G., Mohamed, A., Jaitly, N., Senior, A., Vanhoucke, V., Nguyen, P., Sainath, T.N., Kingsbury, B.: Deep neural networks for acoustic modeling in speech recognition. IEEE Signal Process. Mag. **29**(6), 82–97 (2012)
8. Sainath, T.N., Kingsbury, B., Saon, G., Soltau, H., Mohamed, A.R., Dahl, G., Ramabhadran, B.: Deep convolutional neural networks for large-scale speech tasks. Neural Netw. **64**, 39–48 (2015)
9. Socher, R., Liu, C., Ng, A.: Parsing natural scenes and natural language with recursive neural networks. In: International Conference on Machine Learning (ICML) (2011)
10. Lee, H., Grosse, R., Ranganath, R., Ng, A.Y.: Convolutional deep belief networks for scalable unsupervised learning of hierarchical representations. In: International Conference on Machine Learning (ICML) (2009)
11. Hinton, G.E., Salakhutdinov, R.R.: Reducing the dimensionality of data with neural networks. Science **313**(5786), 504–507 (2006)
12. Hinton, G.E., Osindero, S., Teh, Y.W.: A fast learning algorithm for deep belief nets. Neural Comput. **18**(7), 1527–1554 (2006)
13. Wang, N., Yeung, D.Y.: Learning a deep compact image representation for visual tracking. In: Annual Conference on Neural Information Processing Systems (NIPS) (2013)
14. Vincent, P., Larochelle, H., Lajoie, I., Bengio, Y., Manzagol, P.A.: Stacked denoising autoencoders: learning useful representations in a deep network with a local denoising criterion. J. Mach. Learn. Res. **11**, 3371–3408 (2010)
15. Wu, Y., Lim, J., Yang, M.: Online object tracking: a benchmark. In: IEEE Conference on Computer Vision and Pattern Recognition (CVPR) (2013)
16. Torralba, A., Fergus, R., Freeman, W.T.: 80 Million tiny images: a large data set for nonparametric object and scene recognition. IEEE Trans. Pattern Anal. Mach. Intell. **30**(11), 1958–1970 (2008)
17. Agrawal, P., Girshick, R., Malik, J.: Analyzing the performance of multilayer neural networks for object recognition. In: Fleet, D., Pajdla, T., Schiele, B., Tuytelaars, T. (eds.) ECCV 2014, Part VII. LNCS, vol. 8695, pp. 329–344. Springer, Heidelberg (2014)

18. LeCun, Y., Bengio, Y.: Convolutional networks for images, speech, and time-series. In: Arbib, M.A. (ed.) Handbook of Brain Theory and Neural Networks. MIT Press, Cambridge (1995)
19. Huang, G.B., Lee, H., Erik, L.M.: Learning hierarchical representations for face verification with convolutional deep belief networks. In: IEEE Conference on Computer Vision and Pattern Recognition (CVPR) (2012)
20. Doucet, A., Freitas, D.N., Gordon, N.: Sequential Monte Carlo Methods in Practice. Springer, New York (2001)
21. Arulampalam, M., Maskell, S., Gordon, N., Clapp, T.: A tutorial on particle filters for online nonlinear/non-Gaussian Bayesian tracking. IEEE Trans. Sig. Process. **50**(2), 174–188 (2002)
22. Kalal, Z., Mikolajczyk, K., Matas, J.: Tracking-learning-detection. IEEE Trans. Pattern Anal. Mach. Intell. **34**(7), 1409–1422 (2012)
23. Babenko, B., Yang, M., Belongie, S.: Robust object tracking with online multiple instance learning. IEEE Trans. Pattern Anal. Mach. Intell. **33**(8), 1619–1632 (2011)
24. Ross, D., Lim, J., Lin, R., Yang, M.: Incremental learning for robust visual tracking. Int. J. Comput. Vis. **77**(1), 125–141 (2008)
25. Zhang, K., Zhang, L., Yang, M.-H.: Real-time compressive tracking. In: Fitzgibbon, A., Lazebnik, S., Perona, P., Sato, Y., Schmid, C. (eds.) ECCV 2012, Part III. LNCS, vol. 7574, pp. 864–877. Springer, Heidelberg (2012)
26. Kwon, J., Lee, K.: Visual tracking decomposition. In: IEEE Conference on Computer Vision and Pattern Recognition (CVPR) (2010)
27. Brosch, T., Tam, R.: Efficient training of convolutional deep belief networks in the frequency domain for application to high-resolution 2D and 3D images. Neural Comput. **27**(1), 211–227 (2015)

Author Index

Cai, Guilin 18
Chen, MingYu 1

Dong, Wenrui 18

Gao, Xiang 73

Hu, Dan 103
Hu, Wei 18

Ji, Qing 86
Jiang, Yanhuang 18

Liu, Guangming 18
Liu, Shaoli 45
Lu, Chao 45

Peng, Fei 73

Qi, Kaiyuan 60

Ren, Tong 73

Su, Zhiyuan 60
Sun, GuangYu 1

Tan, Yusong 33

Wang, Jian 45
Wang, Lei 45
Wang, Peng 1
Wang, Qing 73
Wang, Wenzhu 33
Wei, Peng 60
Wu, Junjie 103
Wu, Qingbo 33

Xiao, Junhua 45
Xin, Guomao 60
Xue, Shuangbai 73

Zhang, Dong 60
Zhang, Longbing 45
Zhang, Yaoxue 33
Zhou, Xingshe 103
Zhu, PengFei 1